Willinghol

M.
York C... Girls
1... ...24

by
Margaret Mann Phillips

foreword by
Dame Janet Baker

Highgate Publications (Beverley) Ltd
1989

Editorial Note

Margaret Mann Phillips was concerned not to infringe the privacy of the people mentioned in this book and used pseudonyms to conceal their identities. Because of the passage of time, it has been considered acceptable to substitute the name of the Headmistress, Miss E. E. Ellett, instead of the 'Miss Tarrant' invented by the author, Miss Ellett was known to the girls as 'E-cubed' on account of her initials.

© John Phillips, 1989
   Penelope Phillips, 1989
All Rights Reserved. No part of this publication may be reproduced, stored in a retrieval system, or transmitted, in any form or by any means, electronic, mechanical, photocopying, recording or otherwise without the permission of the copyright owners.

Published by Highgate Publications (Beverley) Ltd.
24 Wylies Road, Beverley, HU17 7AP
Telephone (0482) 866826

Printed and Typeset in 10 on 11pt Plantin by
B.A. Press, 2-4 Newbegin, Lairgate, Beverley, HU17 8EG
Telephone (0482) 882232

British Library Cataloguing in Publication Data

Phillips, Margaret Mann, 1906–1987
   Willingly to school: memories of York College for Girls, 1919–1924.
   1. North Yorkshire. York. Social life, 1901–1936.
   I. Title
   942.8'430823

ISBN 0-948929-23-5

FOREWORD
by Dame Janet Baker

As we grow older the past becomes ever more real and precious to us. It is a delight to share and compare our early memories and to re-discover events as they appear perhaps differently through another's eyes.

At York College, where I spent some very happy years, we were aware in a special sense of the past as it existed all around us in the streets and in our own buildings.

Margaret Mann Phillips would rejoice to see the school still standing in those same streets, just as we rejoice in her telling of the time she spent there.

Janet Baker

PREFACE

My mother wrote this memoir at the request of a friend who asked for a sequel to her memoir of childhood, *Within the City Wall*, which appeared in 1943. The present memoir is a look back at an experience of school life in York just after the First World War, when York College for Girls was in only its second decade of existence. It is therefore naturally of interest to the College, which has so recently celebrated its eightieth anniversary.

However, for my mother it was not solely a matter of looking back. In her narrative she shows us the germ of her future career which was planted during those years at the College. Her first 'meeting' with Erasmus is recounted here, as is her first impression of Oxford. In her diary for 26 April 1921, she wrote: 'Mother and I went to Oxford. It's the nicest place I've ever been to, just like heaven. The ... glorious buildings like palaces, and ... the boys in gowns and girls in square caps like Portia!'

Perhaps fittingly, it was in Oxford that she died, in 1987. She missed the College's eightieth birthday celebrations, but she would be pleased that by means of this memoir she can still have a part in them.

Penelope Phillips
September 1989

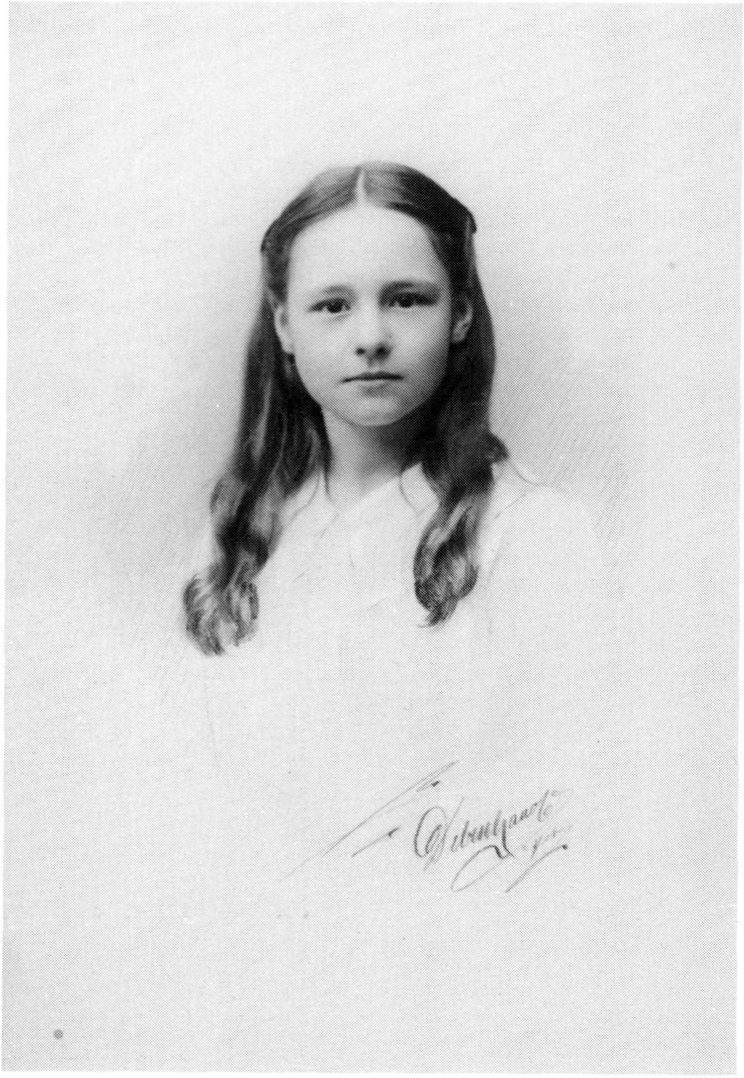

Chapter One

First Term

I

Dear friend, you want to know something about my early life....You were pleased with the account of my twelve-year-old existence 'within the City wall', and for years you have asked for more. But the description of a precise, balanced period like childhood is one thing; to speak of adolescence is, I find, *autrement difficile.* Childhood looks outward as well as inward and sees a new world; adolescence sees nothing so important in life as itself. To consider such a self-centred stage without egotism, but without cynicism either, is plainly walking the tightrope.

You set me a hard task, but one not without interest. Everyone has a valid experience, all life is interesting, even a life almost without external events has its drama and its conflict. Above all, youth has the perspective of its *possible* fulfilments to enlarge the narrow canvas. The five years I have tried to portray were simple in outline, quiet on the surface, not unusual or disturbed. Nevertheless, they held all the shadowy imprint of those elements which uplift or terrify or imperil the youth of a more violent day.

★★★

You remember, of course, the tall Victorian front of the Rectory with its step-gable and round eyes at the top and its square bay window and four steps up to the front door at the bottom. And the long walk from there to the poor parish 'within the City wall' with its varied life in the narrow streets, and the old road that runs through it across the River Foss to the great towers of the Minster, glimpsed grey and splendid between the slanting roofs and jutting house-fronts of mediaeval York. All the amalgam of past and present that had woven such a rich tapestry for me as a child was still there — but now I was to see life differently.

1919; the War was over, and I was thirteen. Up to that time I had never been to school. Or more precisely, I had attended a small school run by my music-teacher for a period of a few weeks. Money was scarce at the Rectory but resources were many. My parents must have had the Victorian view that a girl learnt best at home, and they took over my education. I remember that, when it became a serious consideration, my mother made out a timetable: English, painting, history, geography, arithmetic, even French. The English and the painting progressed happily because she loved them; I was an apt pupil for the English and a dutiful one for art. But arithmetic was painful, history came out of *Little Arthur's England*, and geography was contained in a thin dark-covered book consisting of question and answer: *e.g. What is an isthmus?* French got no further than an astonished discovery of genders. The other aspect of teaching was my father's Latin. It was hard but I struggled to please him, and we got on well with Dr. Smith's grammar and exercises, pronouncing in the old English way: *filii*, as in magpie. It seemed unlikely that the case-structure would ever become second nature; but one ceased to wonder at it in time.

Otherwise I read. And what did I read? I learnt to read at my mother's knee at the age of four, and the house was full of books. There were books of my own, given by more or less discerning relations, and other people of my generation will recognise these. Some were considered suitable for my instruction, with titles like *Faith Gartney's Girlhood* or *From Log-Cabin to White House*. Also in this category were the works of Amy Lefeuvre (*Bunny's Friends, Probable Sons, etc*). Some of these books, now obscure, were read and re-read by both my brother and myself: *Beyond the Blue Mountains*, for instance, and *His Great Opportunity* — books with discoverable morals but also a good story. My godmother had a run of Mrs Ewing, whose books are delightful to this day. It is remarkable how many of the best children's books were American: *Little Women*, of course, and the *Wide, Wide World* and its sequel, *Ellen Montgomery's Bookshelf*. A fine story, much-maligned, was *Little Lord Fauntleroy* and that has an American beginning. However, even this paled before *The Secret Garden*, surely the best children's story ever written. I had an odd interest in that classic of an earlier day, *Ministering Children*. Weightier books found their way to me. My father's mother, gentle Granny, gave me a Shakespeare when I was nine; and his favourite sister, Auntie Clara, a *Gateway to Chaucer*, with lovely pictures. My other godmother, beloved Auntie Sarah, sent me the *Girl's Own Paper* year after year, a production I hated — but I loved her too much to tell her so. My brother's *Boy's Own Paper* was much more in my line. In fact, boys' books were the best — like *The Coral Island*. But by the time this story begins I should have said my favourite books were *Westward Ho!* and *Henry Esmond*.

There were, however, other categories of reading matter: that which was to be found in my father's study and on my mother's bookshelf. The study was a long tunnel-like room with two round-headed windows at one end. On that side the shelves which lined the room held mostly theology, with an encyclopaedia on the floor level (the volumes were personified to us children by their mysterious names, *A-Bak* to *Tab-Zym*). Then came the fireplace over which a few tiny volumes had a niche. And then a wall full of miscellaneous books of all descriptions. I browsed...

My mother's bookshelf was in the dining-room. Two small shelves, some twenty books in good bindings, black and red like those treasured by Chaucer's *Clerk of Oxenford* (only there were green and gold ones too). They were eighteenth and nineteenth century poets: Goldsmith, Young, Scott, Moore, Southey, Hood, Wordsworth, Shelley, Byron, Coleridge, Browning, Longfellow. I dipped. With Longfellow and Tennyson it was more than dipping: I lived with them, with Tennyson's gravity and classic mediaevalism, with Longfellow's early American and wide European sympathies. Very early in life I had been entranced by my mother's reading of *The Courtship of Miles Standish*. There was another American book there too, in a couple of little paperbacks: *The Autocrat of the Breakfast Table*. That was read over and over again and gave me an unexplained delight. My mother's bookshelf was small but its influence was incalculable.

However, there came a time when something else had to be done. My brother had gone through the whole process of kindergarten, prep-school, public school and now was just on the point of going to Oxford. I was experiencing a strange slump in vitality. From the excitement and widening horizons of being twelve I had faded into the lethargy and lack of interest of being thirteen. There seemed nowhere to go in life. This was no doubt partly physical growth. It could not possibly occur to me that the whole nation was feeling like I was, the ebullience of Armistice Day having faded into the foggy dampness of the post-war period ('a world fit for heroes to live in'). What affected me was that at this point my parents began to talk about school.

They toyed with the idea of boarding-school, but it was too expensive. My father went to see the headmistress of the College. I can imagine their interview. Miss Ellett had been headmistress for some years now, ever since the High School had removed from its old place in a square house near my home to blossom out as the College under the guidance of the Church Schools Company in a large formal house in a busy narrow street near the Minster. In that small high-ceilinged office just inside the front door my fate was decided. I can see Miss Ellett (a mathematician, known to the school as *T-squared*) turning round from her desk, iron-grey hair and pince-nez giving her dignity, to face the new parent, whose hair was prematurely white and his eyes blue and twinkling in a fine mobile face.

What she learnt from him presented something of a problem. His daughter had apparently grown to thirteen without formal schooling, had read a great deal and was always writing, had no French but quite a lot of Latin; her mathematics were poor and old-fashioned in method but her acquaintance with English literature unusual; her history and geography merely accidental, practically non-existent. Of elementary science she had no inkling at all. How was she to be fitted into any form without Procrustean methods?

Miss Ellett said that the French, or lack of it, was the greatest drawback. She had mentioned it to her French mistress, who had nobly volunteered to give the child some coaching before term began. No, there would be no fee to pay. Miss Elmbridge was ready to help in this difficult case. The Rector thanked her, wondering perhaps what kind of present he could offer to this devoted woman when her act of kindness was over.

And so I began a fortnight's real study, riding from the Rectory to the flat Miss Elmbridge occupied on the other side of the city. It meant a longer bicycle ride than I had been used to do alone, through the busy streets, avoiding the tramlines and skirting Walmgate Bar to circle Foss Islands, veering uncertainly at the far end into a district I had hardly visited before, coming closer to the big chocolate factory (Rowntree's) with its delicious smell. The house where Miss Elmbridge lived was a genteel terrace-house, with a bay window on the ground floor and one over it; the kind of house you could not imagine without an aspidistra.

Inside the first-floor room with the bay window I found myself sitting opposite the first schoolmistress I had ever met, except my aforementioned anxious little music-teacher. I was somewhat awestruck. There was nothing terrifying about Miss Elmbridge, but she was my new teacher and when she looked at me with kindly eyes from under the severe locks of hair unfashionably looped up on each side of her central parting, and suggested, 'You might learn as much as you can of this verb', I took her quite literally and learnt it all. Miss Elmbridge successfully concealed her surprise. She was used to sales resistance and did not succeed with large classes. In this case she said nothing and gave me twice as much to learn next time. In this way we got through quite a substantial amount of French grammar in the fortnight.

How pleasant those lessons were! One result of home education was that I had never had, nor apparently needed, much physical freedom. I had no sense of imprisonment, though I did occasionally wish I could stand in the garden and yell with all my lungs — obviously it would not do, people would come running — and I even eyed the milkman's float with his docile pony and wondered what would happen if I stepped on to the low floor and took the reins and sped off down the road like Ben-Hur driving his chariot. But it never happened. Those days when I had written in my diary *You think I'm a girl, but I'm really a boy, and my chief qualities are mischievousness, recklessness, daring* were over. I was reconciled as far as I knew to a life where one's coming and goings were witnessed, one's explorations entirely in the mind. But now one came and went and there was a chink of bliss to be out alone in the sleepy afternoon, free-wheeling down the road towards the river, skirting the cattle-pens clustered under the green mound of the Wall, pedalling past the Bar with its barbican and along the line of the Foss where the Red Tower ended the fortifications and past the immense flour-mill which stood black against the sky. After crossing the Foss, a quiet tree-lined road ran along outside the stretch of Wall which enclosed the Roman legionary fort. This was Lord Mayor's Walk (less quiet now, alas) and there, particularly on the way home, I would slow down and put a toe to the ground, balance against one of the lamp-posts and pull out a little volume from my pocket. Oddly enough, it was here that I savoured the full ecstasy of being alone, reading Rossetti in the September sunlight which filtered between the branches, while a triumphant voice said in my heart *Nobody knows where I am.*

Miss Elmbridge did not know quite what to make of her new scholar. She asked questions and got answers she did not expect, untouched by fashions of classroom or playground. When she asked, 'Who is your favourite author?' and I answered firmly, 'Thackeray,' (on the strength of one book only, *Henry Esmond*), her eyes widened. 'Not Dickens?' To this I responded by remarking that life was difficult because one never knew what people were thinking, and it would be a much better arrangement if they had windows in their heads or chests — I wasn't sure which. Miss Elmbridge's eyes crinkled up in her head with laughter so that they made straight lines in her face like a cat. 'Oh, I don't think that would do at all!'

For both teacher and pupil it was a honeymoon of learning. I found out later that Miss Elmbridge was used to fighting her way through French lessons, keeping down the restless spirits or vainly shoving forward the bored and inattentive ones. For a couple of weeks she taught in enjoyment and peace, and I learnt with curiosity and without fatigue. I was just at the point where parrot-learning was a pleasure, and had not yet given place to associative memory. Another year or two and French verbs would not have had their repetitive charm. I was lucky.

However, the fortnight came to an end and the first day of term arrived. The rest of the family must have considered this new venture in their different ways. My brother was just starting his last year at public school. The educational gamut went a long way back for him and perhaps he thought it was just as well that I had not been thrust into the boarding-school experience. He seemed Olympian to me; from thirteen to eighteen the gap is enormous, and I did not expect him to notice my humble beginnings. I was proud of him, though, and gratified ever to be invited to share in his concerns.

Daddy was always active and busy in his parish, but equally always particularly interested in his children's affairs. His buoyant optimism could have anticipated no difficulties about this late entry into school, especially as he had an idea I was not slow to learn, but this was a carefully-guarded secret. His was a hopeful and confident nature, but it was more than that — it was really as if he felt his hand in the hand of God. He said to me once, unforgettably, 'I think you'll be like me — you'll always get what you want.'

I never wanted anything in my life that I didn't get.' And then after a moment's reflection he added with great simplicity, 'Of course I never wanted anything I oughtn't to have.'

Mother had a sixth sense as far as her children were concerned. She looked at them with the eye of prescience. One knew that whatever happened one could be sure of a quiet hearing, complete understanding and a practical suggestion. Or indeed it might be that an acute psychological explanation of the circumstances which had hurt would cancel out the sting. This wonderful skill had been developed over the years.

In our early childhood she had been strict. Long afterwards I found out that this was her great regret. But it came from a high standard of what we must be and a deep sense of her responsibility. Through watching and longing and praying she found out the secret of love: to be on the other person's side. Whatever happened, whatever had gone wrong, mother would be on one's side. She would apply her rigorous standards of integrity to what one had done, but she would always understand why one had done it.

Mother was probably anxious about my going to school; she became particularly watchful. But she entered into the preparations with capable efficiency.

The girl who lived across the road was already in the Sixth Form; she would soon be eighteen. It was a real kindness on her part to consent to a child's company on the way to school — or so I felt it to be. Of course, it may have been difficult to refuse, as she had known me since I was three, but it must have struck her that I was a potential nuisance.

The way to school was through the centre of the town, a shortish bicycle ride but hampered by a certain amount of traffic congestion. The motor-car was just taking over from the horse, but there were still many horse-drawn cabs and carts in the streets. It was possible and pleasant then to be a reckless cyclist. I eventually used to do the journey in five minutes, darting under the outstretched arm of the policeman on point duty when my brakes refused to work. Once I tipped into a wheelbarrow because I had not taken my eyes off the profile of the Minster. On another occasion I skidded on the wet tramlines and went home with a split chin. Nevertheless, I had remarkably few accidents.

On this first occasion I imagine we proceeded cautiously. It was a little embarrassing to see my old friend, the Sixth Form girl, through junior eyes; it felt queer to wear my new green serge gym tunic with the three box pleats swinging from a velvet yoke, and my new green blazer with the proud badge which was the Minster's too. On my head, the same badge adorned the green ribbon round the black velour hat, and the elastic which kept it on was new and tight. Long brown stockings, woolly and scratchy behind the knees, completed the outfit. It was the exciting equipment for a new life, soon to become normal, but never disliked.

The handsome house which contained the school was a gentleman's residence in the eighteenth century, altered in the nineteenth, and joined on to older buildings, whose Tudor gables backed on to a strange old church. The frontage of the school consisted of a large imposing porch (imposing to me) standing on its three stone steps above the level of the street, and a tall frontage behind it, with a tradesmen's entrance opening on to a little flagged yard. This was the pupils' entrance if they came on foot. Next door, as tightly clamped to the building as possible, old fronts pushed out bow windows to the narrow street where a variety of humble traders, greengrocers, toy merchants and bakers, made their livings. One sold brass objects and another had a full-sized plaster Napoleon taking snuff outside its door and an old figure of a cheerful savage in a grass skirt perched high up on the wall.

Only parents and visitors entered by the front door. Pupils, if they arrived on bicycles, turned the corner and approached the school from the back. This meant dismounting and pushing one's machine through the short alley finished by posts, called Minster Gate. Every day for terms and terms that particular aspect of the Minster was to rise in front of me: the high south porch on its throne of steps, the familiar lancet windows of the south transept and the foliated rose, the choir with one tall bay jutting out splendidly like a wall of glass, and the great watchful mass of the central tower behind. I was not much acquainted with the terms of architecture, but I had an inkling that this belonged to the time most familiar to me through my childish enthusiasms — and called itself *Perpendicular*.

The Minster was always in the background, and wove itself into the stuff of one's thoughts. It was tremendous, awe-inspiring and unbelievable, and yet quite familiar, like a mixture of a mountain landscape and a pet animal.

We walked our bicycles up the lane between backs of houses and the choirboys' playing field, and in through a green door into the school garden. At the time it had not long ceased to be a real garden of a town house, and at one end there was an artificial mound, perhaps builders' rubble or, perhaps, had I but known it, the old fashion of a *Mount* in a garden, dating from the Renaissance. Most of the garden was turfed, and there were bicycle sheds along the wall and in front of the basement kitchens. The house was frankly Victorian on this side and adorned with two pepper-pot turrets. The Sixth Form girl showed me the way to the cloakroom where there would be a peg bearing my name, and disappeared into more distinguished regions.

The cloakroom had an unforgettable smell, not unpleasant and not merely antiseptic. It smelt of shoes, indiarubber, and floor-polish. I changed my shoes, hung them up in the green bag embroidered with my initials by my mother, added my hat and blazer, and watched the other girls who came in chattering and fell silent after a giggle or two; talking in the cloakroom was forbidden.

A bell rang, and we filed out under the eye of a prefect; it happened to be the same Sixth Form girl, who gave me a cool little smile as I passed by. And so into the hall of the old house, which was clean and bare in its cream and white paint, and into the large room which had no doubt been a dining-room before two rooms were thrown into one: a pleasant place looking on to the garden, with long French windows and a round alcove under the pepper-pot tower. After a few minutes the headmistress came in and stood at her reading-desk. She gave out the number of a hymn.

'Lord, behold us with Thy blessing,' sang the school, 'Once again assembled here.'

But for me it was the first time, and I looked about me at the rows of faces, the heads flaxen, dark or chestnut, the enviably straight noses, the rosy cheeks, confident lips, bright critical eyes. They all knew each other; what chance was there for a newcomer? And they wouldn't want to know *me* anyway, I thought. Yet, although so alarming, it was also exciting to be there, among people of my own age for the first time.

These enviable beings were called by the names of their generation: *Dorothy, Rosemary, Evelyn, Phyllis*... In a few years their places would be taken by young women bearing such names as *Zena, Shirley* or *Mavis;* or perhaps, with a return to simplicity, *Susan* or *Jane;* or, with a new bias towards the classics, *Olivia, Claudia, Penelope*...

I had leisure now to look at the headmistress's face. T-squared was not the emaciated scholarly type. She had full cheeks and a high colour, an eagle's nose — and eyes that looked straight at you from behind her pince-nez. There was courage in that face and mastery; also devastating sarcasm and swift judgement. She was not an easy person and every line of her meant clear purpose and determination. The girls started by being afraid of her; but it soon became clear to them that she could be considerate, respectful of their individualities and utterly just.

Beside her there stood a row of mistresses. Someone told me that the little sandy one was the Latin teacher; a thin dark one stood next to a red-faced jolly one; and then came Miss Elmbridge, whose bowed head wore the usual bird's nest of hair and whose grey cardigan and flat shoes were a heartening and recognisable sight.

There were others, but the distinctive figure of the group was the tall, ascetic person with the quiet face — wide forehead, dark centre-parted hair, grey serene eyes — and this, as I knew from my Sixth Form friend, was the revered second mistress, Miss Steele.

The school began singing a psalm. *I was glad when they said unto me, we will go up into the house of the Lord. Our feet shall stand within thy gates, O Jerusalem.* Surely that might mean the Minster? My eyes sought the high skyline of grey crockets that could be seen from the assembly-room window. *For my brethren and companions' sakes, I will wish thee prosperity. Yea, for the sake of the house of the Lord our God, I will seek to do thee good.*

Every first day of term for five years I was to sing that psalm and begin a new chapter of life under the watching presence of that familiar giant — my version of Jerusalem.

II

The Fourth Form of that day was a room overlooking the small paved area outside the kitchens (now a housekeeper's rooms). It faced into the garden, but the bay window looking north-east was darkened by the protruding angle of the house. Smells of school dinner floated up to it. It was a conveniently square room but not a cheerful one, retaining the perennial smell of indiarubber and old desks.

My own desk was in the front row against the wall, so near the door that when jobs were allocated it necessarily fell to me to be ready to open and close the door when teachers came and went. I would guess that the older or more longstanding pupils were given superior status by having seats at the back of the room. The desk had a sloping lid with deep furrowed initials carved on it; the patterns they made were to grow familiar and I was to add my share, deepening them by gouging with a pencil in odd moments. Between the desk and the door hung a baize-covered notice-board, and in the corner near the bay-window, on my left, the mistress's desk sat squarely on its platform.

New books were handed out and we tidied them away.

'Not so much noise, *please!*' The form mistress — the little sandy-haired Latin teacher — peered rather helplessly through short-sighted eyes at the lid-banging crowd in front of her. The girl next to me nudged her neighbour and with a cackle of laughter showed her one of the pictures in the geography textbook. I caught a glimpse of it — some kind of tribal dance. It set them both off in snorts of giggling.

Why did I stiffen — with real dread in my heart? I think it was because that laugh touched the spring of fear which I had been conscious of ever since I knew I was to go to school. There was a kind of refusal in those snorts, some gibe at the whole business of learning. This attitude existed, I knew, and maybe it was contagious. And then one might lose the world of imagination. Possibly I did not articulate this fear to myself very clearly at the time. But the effect of years of reading had been to make that world the most real of all worlds to me. What the drawbacks might be to living in a mental country peopled by *Amyas Leigh* and *Hereward the Wake*, the prince of the *Golden Legend* or Tennyson's *Arthur*, 'vext with waste dreams', the dry smile of Colonel Esmond or the backwoods downrightness of Miles Standish, I could not tell, but it was a heroic atmosphere and I was unwilling to lose it. No doubt there were other countries of the mind too and these were all somehow denied by that laugh. So I sat silently and awkwardly in my desk, priggishly maybe, certainly on the defensive, while the chatter and giggling which the form mistress was unable to quell went on surging round me.

At the appointed time she scuttled away; and I held the door open for the next teacher. As her step was heard in the corridor the unruliness faded from the room. The girls standing by their desks became quite silent. The gaunt figure of Miss Steele was now at the mistress's desk. She had no need to 'keep order': her personality did that for her. She had been at the school when it was the old High School, before its removal to the house I was coming to know; she was an older hand even than T-squared. The girls thought she was a saint, and before her level gaze their smaller selves seemed to acquire the power of concentration, thereby becoming more important. She did not dwarf you but made you feel you could do what she expected — and she expected a great deal.

Miss Steele told us we were to read *The Tempest*. I looked at the exercise books I had been given: they were really beautiful, large and flat with bright glossy colours, pink and blue, turquoise and chocolate. The one which was to hold my English essays was orange. I stroked it with pleasure, enjoying the extraordinary charm of paper. And all those blank pages inside!

When Miss Steele was replaced by Miss Elmbridge, who had tutored me in French, the atmosphere again changed. Standing in front of the class with her arms folded, a characteristic pose, in her grey cardigan and striped blouse with the high neck already out of fashion, she directed us to open our French grammars and to start learning verbs. A groan went up.

'But we've been through it twice already!' My neighbour sounded mutinous.

As for me, since I had never been through it even once, I had no share in the universal disgust. It was nothing to me that Miss Elmbridge always wore the same clothes and expected an idle class to imbibe French the hard way, and suffered the resistance with irritating resignation. Her methods may have been old-fashioned. Had it been a more efficient way of learning basic French grammar to pack it into a fortnight instead of spreading it over six years? Anyway, I could learn from Miss Elmbridge and the boost I got from that first earlier forcing into the world of school never lost its impetus. Later, I was to discover that there were a few other people on Miss Elmbridge's side.

The bell rang and there followed a breathless interval, of which I could only be a stunned spectator, called 'Rec'. I stood against the garden wall and watched the groups of girls running or sauntering, meeting, mingling and dividing again: it was like standing on the edge of a world within a world. On the other side of the grass plot a group of Olympian seniors was in discussion. I observed one of the group detach herself and cross over to me: it was the Sixth Form girl.

'How are you getting on?' she asked.

I looked up gratefully — for Winifred was tall — into the pale charming face with the grey eyes and tilted nose and humorous mouth, all framed in dark, dark shining curls. I had never seen her so clearly before. I mumbled something, unable to respond adequately to this mark of condescension. Winifred looked at me mischievously; then the bell rang.

Back in the classroom, I held the door open for T-squared, who swept into the room with an air of tremendous purpose. There was no lid-banging now, no rebellious murmurings; every head was bent over the theorem or the equation. T-squared was not one to suffer fools gladly. *Close your eyes with holy dread!*

If a girl did not grasp mathematical principles, T-squared could not believe it was simply due to incapacity: such things were so clear to her! It was obviously merely indolence or a wilful refusal to concentrate. She felt she could be justly severe. Her sharp irony was feared by the whole school. The fact that she did not spare herself, that the standards of discipline which she applied to all were applied to herself too, gave a great power to her impact on the young. My attempts at arithmetic had been a puzzled introduction to a mystery, my mother's methods being those of an older generation, quite different from T-squared's. I floundered hopelessly, and she looked at me with amazed exasperation. Fortunately for me, at this early stage her reaction merely took the form of silent despair.

Midday. Somewhere in the corridor a clock was striking. The class rose to its feet. Quite still, the girls stood at attention beside their desks, as the largest of the Minster's bells, Great Peter, boomed out twelve slow strokes that vibrated in the air. One felt one would never forget that sound; it penetrated every crevice of the body and died away echoing in the heart, a great completeness packed into its sheaf of chords. The ceremony was a legacy from the War, when the school had devoted the space of those twelve strokes to prayer. Now, in 1919, they still rose to their feet to honour the dead.

III

I soon found I had a hard row to hoe. It was perplexing to be so different from the others. Some things with which they had been familiar for years were quite new to me, and it was difficult to gauge clearly the extent and cause of my discomfort.

It was not only the different forms of maths which foxed me; there was geography, almost a blank page. And there was history: my notions of that were miscellaneous — a host of 'backgrounds' to favourite books, incompletely understood, a frequent stare at a genealogical table of the Kings of England (a treasured possession and pretty accurate, though it did start at Woden) and a secret detailed study of the years 1485-7 for the historical novel I had tried to write. This preparation was hardly sufficient.

Then there was science. The science teacher was a jolly-looking character whose appearance suggested farming rather than the laboratory. Stories lingered on about her classes and the patience she had displayed with the previous generation, wild daughters of war, who had thought nothing of making whoopee in the lab. and sliding down the passages primed with pink soap. Her classes were still rather chaotic, and mysterious as to their aims, though it appeared one could get good marks by drawing neat pictures of test-tubes and retorts, and Bunsen flames in three colours.

In French I was still behind the others, but catching up fast because I was not bored with the grammar. In Latin my father's lessons actually put me in front; but how confusing it was to have to substitute a new pronunciation — so that *O filii* and *filiae* came out exactly the other way round!

There were also some other areas where I was ahead. For example, my home had given me some knowledge of the Bible. And, indeed, in the use of the English language it was fortunate that I had *not* been at school. Education was just then having one of its fashionable lapses about teaching grammar, but my mother had the methods of an earlier age, and I had been drilled in parsing until the parts of speech were old friends.

In English literature my knowledge was unorganised and past selections wildly arbitrary — but they had included some of the best. Mother had introduced me to Milton; I had read simplified versions of certain Shakespeare plays and some of *The Canterbury Tales*, as well as from my beloved complete Shakespeare. Browsing had yielded such books as *The Vicar of Wakefield*, and the old anthology on my father's shelves, *Aikin's Poets*, had opened with Ben Jonson's *Hymn to Diana* with its incandescent flash, *Goddess excellently bright...*

There had also been odd volumes resulting from my father's frequent visits to the second-hand bookstall in the market-place. (I understood later that the reason why this stall always had a copy of *Telemaque*, in French or English, was that so many gentlemen's libraries were coming on sale at this time. If only one had been a real collector!) Some homage must be paid here to the contribution of Arthur Mee and his *Children's Encyclopaedia* and *Children's Magazine*. These enriched a whole generation.

The problem was that, to me, English literature was a wild woodland where one roamed — not a subject for study. Thus, I was as much out of step with the others here as in the rest of the work despite the fact that I was old in experience instead of being completely blank and green.

Then there were games — a strange phenomenon. I had never played an organised game in my life and was quite at sea, standing in front of the goal at hockey while the game went on at the opposite end of the field until the unguarded moment when it made an unexpected rush at me, recalling me from watching the shapes of the elms against the winter sunset and wondering when it would be time to go home. Or leaping about at netball, trying to understand what the teacher meant when she shouted, 'Mark your opponent!' (a phrase never explained). Everybody else had learnt the jargon long ago. They all knew the six Scottish dancing steps, could all climb ropes and do handstands, while my untrained body would not spring or bend. But I am sure no one ever jeered; that would have been unthinkable. The games mistress was a wonderful character, short and stocky with a face like Napoleon, and she kept the school under discipline like a sergeant-major. The respect accorded to her was universal, but there was no need to be afraid of her — she knew when one was really trying.

The greatest indignity was that the teaching staff objected to my handwriting. I had started to write with old-fashioned copy-books and had developed a scrawl, which had not improved during the years since I was eight, spent mainly on writing. The school authorities decided that I must start all over again. With rebellion in my heart I spent miserable afternoons copying the new script-writing which everyone else had learnt.

The models to copy were quotations; one particularly infuriated me: *Men must work and women must weep.* Without a context this roused active feminism. Somehow, out of a home which worked on a basis of perfect understanding between parents, I had grown up with a passionate sense that life was unjust to women. Was it because my mother's genius in domestic matters, which reduced mountains of work to an imperceptible routine, was in my eyes founded on abnegation? I was little use to her, though she managed to give me enough ideas about housekeeping to meet my needs later on. But she had given up trying about the time of the beginning of this story. My lack of interest must have been disheartening.

The rest of the form must have been as nonplussed by me as I by them. The rush of selfconsciousness resultant on being plunged into group life made me take it for granted that I would remain an outsider, and it seemed to me a matter of destiny. I was great on destiny. Perhaps Arthur Mee is to blame here — I remember a caption to a picture of a mother sitting beside a cradle:

> *Thou mayest be Christ or Shakespeare, little child,*
> *A saviour or a sun to this lost world.*

But also it was the result of being alone. Solitary children have time to recognise the uniqueness of their path; and one's path really is unique. A strong sense of being intended for some particular line of events was always present to me, and perhaps this is what *group* education misses. Life always wore a mysterious, enigmatic face, but it was a face of hope; great things were to be done, growing was meaningful. Perhaps the blankness of the future for so many young people of a later generation is a reflection of the blankness of their present. Cut up by the incursions of other personalities, by competing sets of ideas and multiple views of the world thrust upon them by artificial means, they never have the silence that is needed for a gathering of strength from their own inner resources. And not even from just their own, maybe; a silence opens the door on the infinite sea.

Special misery were the drawing lessons when, under the indulgent eye of a kindly elderly teacher, the girls pushed their chairs together, held their drawing-boards close to one another, chattered and gossiped and drew, when they felt like it, a still-life group arranged on a table or a box to teach perspective. They were not unkind. Sometimes one of them would invite me to draw my chair alongside, but at the beginning I was too shy or too sure I would be taking someone else's place. They left it at that and stopped making social efforts. One day, the wag of the form, a pleasant square-faced girl with long pigtails, was sitting next to me; it must have been a day when the feeling of being left out was strong, otherwise I would surely not have said to her in a felonious attempt to find out what they really thought:

'I'm partly Scottish, you see, that's why I'm so *dour.*'

The wag responded innocently, 'Oh, is it?' confirming my supposition that they found me queer — and then seeing the trap added quickly and kind-heartedly, 'But you aren't *really*, you know.'

The emotional shock produced by this late transplanting from home to school gave me thus a temporary likeness to an immortal character of fiction yet unborn — Eeyore. But it was apparently confirmed by a storm which blew up over the English essays.

The form became aware, as term went on, that their tranquillity of mind was threatened. Accustomed to a shared indifference to the bees in the bonnets of the teachers, including their bizarre requests for homework, they were really perturbed to find a blackleg in their midst — someone unaware of the usual subterfuges of school life who took the teachers at their word. This 'keenness' did not matter in most subjects because the blackleg was far behind, but in English it created a troublesome situation. The school was not strongly competitive; it was small and comprehensive in terms of mixed ability. This was good and there was a blessed absence at this stage of exam fever; the School Certificate was far away in the future, two years at least. Nevertheless, it might be said that there was a certain degree of placidity.

Miss Steele accepted my essays non-committally and did not mark them very high. She did engage in a battle with me about my curious habit of leaving the top line of each page blank. There was nothing unusual about my efforts except perhaps a greater awareness of punctuation and a rather more grown-up vocabulary than she found in the others. But one day she tried to infuse more vigour into the tone of schoolgirl writing in general.

'Take this from your own personal angle, try to take it in a new way,' she said.

One ear heard. After years of writing with encouragement but without criticism, it occurred to me to do what she seemed to want. The essay was to be on *The Tempest,* Act 2, Scene 2, which is the meeting between Caliban and the drunken jester and butler, Trinculo and Stephano. When the lesson came round which was to give us back our orange exercise-books, she kept the pile on the desk beside her.

'Most of you took no notice of what I said,' she chided us gently. 'Do you remember? I said it was not a summary of the scene that I wanted, not just an account of what happened. I wanted you to think what it *meant*. Only one of you tried to do this. Listen...'

Miss Steele was wise and experienced; she mentioned no name. That was her way. I had enjoyed writing the essay because her words had been an illumination to me, and it was with astonishment that I heard my own phrases read out. To be invited to exercise judgement was a new thing. I had been electrified to realise that Caliban and the two men were on different planes. Caliban was evil but also the one with the poetry, made of other stuff from mortals; while Trinculo and Stephano were merely people, humdrum and sordid. It struck me like a sudden light that it was Caliban who had the lines of high and simple poetry to say; he was above the others and also beneath them, monstrous but immortal; his ugliness held beauty, while they were just clay. It was the first time any such idea had entered my mind.

The class heard the essay read in unreceptive silence. At the end a voice from the back said defensively, 'Oh, I didn't know we were allowed to *criticise* Shakespeare!'

Miss Steele sighed and went on with the lesson.

When it was over, I held the door open for her and she left the classroom. As I stood behind the door waiting for the next arrival, a figure loomed up before me. It was one of the girls I had as yet hardly spoken to and who had certainly never taken any notice of me before.

'Did you write that essay?' she asked accusingly.

Naively, I admitted that I had. It had been good to be praised — what was wrong with that? I had no idea of the trouble in the hearts of my fellow pupils.

Later that week I was summoned by the prefect.

'The girls say you are spending too much time on your homework,' she explained. 'They say it's unfair. We aren't supposed to spend more than half an hour on each subject, don't you know that? If there are four subjects, that's two hours. They want me to tell you that you are not to spend any more time than the others do — half an hour. So be careful.'

Half an hour? Could one write an essay in half an hour with one's eye on the clock? Was it true that other people could dictate one's actions, measure out one's time, decide how much one was to learn or to write about something one loved? So they had had a council on the subject, arranging what I was to be told and how I was to be made to conform! It was my first experience of restrictive practices and I found it shattering.

The prefect was not the leader of a gang. In fact, she was a gentle girl who later became a missionary; she must have felt she was only fulfilling instructions and this without animus. The half-hour restriction was a genuine one, established by the headmistress herself. The fact remained that I was disapproved of and my intellectual liberty threatened. Doing one's best could blacken one in the eyes of someone else.

The dejection I carried home with me could not escape the eyes of my mother. It was not long before I had explained what had happened; with the explanation came long-repressed tears. They were not for this incident only but arose from a train of experiences of which this was but the culmination. My mother paused in her ironing and looked at me with those deep soft brown eyes which saw everything. She never overpraised her children but was quick with protection in their hour of need.

'I'm not surprised,' she said. 'They're jealous, of course — but they don't know it. That's how people behave when they are jealous and afraid. Never mind, they'll get over it. If this is a rule you must try to keep it, but do your work well all the same. It's never being unfair to do your best.'

Incomparable ally, to whose breast all one's troubles could be consigned, who always managed to give one back self-respect without putting one against the world! Seen through her eyes, the injustices of others or one's own clumsiness were explicable and remediable. Told to her, all repentances were fragrant, all fears were groundless, all ambitions pure.

The Rectory, Fulford Road, now part of the Priory Hotel. (By courtesy of the Priory Hotel)

Chapter Two
Home Interlude

The term moved slowly along, then quickened up at the end. This time it really meant something to have Christmas holidays. They had of course always spelt certain things: the return of John from school with the regained feeling of a complete family unit, the anxious planning for Christmas presents, the descent from the North of Grandma.

John's return was exciting even though he seemed so much further on in life as to be almost beyond reach. However, his coming set a livelier tempo; the artistic instincts he had inherited from both parents came into play with leisure, and the house was full of music.

Without question I gave back to him the bedroom which had always been his, the small one next to my parents' room, and climbed the steep stairs to the attic with the dormer window where I now slept, alone on the top floor since a living-in maid had become a mere memory. I had little affection for that bedroom; it was dark, since the tiny dormer was awkwardly placed at one side, and there was nothing in it but a chest of drawers topped by a mirror, an old washstand that was never used, and a few pegs on the wall. But the westward view was beautiful; high over the town gardens the great elm trees fretted the sky, with crossing branches making those shapes that are so characteristic of elms; and the presence of the unseen river beyond them was like a fragrance in darkness.

Next door, the long room overlooking the street, with its large window and two portholes, was still a playroom, and most of John's drawings must have been done there. Two other small rooms, communicating, completed the top floor. I was to inhabit them all in turn, but in 1919 I was still a child in the old bedroom, rather cut off from light and life below, but accepting this as one of the endurances that gave one fortitude.

There were moments when it was needed, and they had often seemed to me like training. The old vague fears of childhood had passed away and in their place came more precise ones linked to the future — what if one went mad...or had an incurable disease? Sometimes it was easy to imagine one of these things could happen. The treatment was to get out of bed, kneel at the

The front entrance of York College.

bedside with a shivering back turned to the shadowy door and dark staircase from which anything hostile might erupt, and say one's prayers. I was a believer in the efficacy of prayer (a belief which later life has consolidated). To pray against the demons and then to hand over the situation to the Lord and climb back into bed fortified and ready to rest was a natural proceeding.

It might have been supposed that my father with all his cares for the household of God would neglect his own. Nothing could have been further from the truth. But certainly Christmas time found him immersed in his poor parish, intent on producing a season of joy for everyone in it, scattering small benefits which sometimes came from the church charities and sometimes from his own pocket, arranging here for a bag of coal and there for a rabbit for the Christmas dinner, or the small sum of money that would make all the difference. He was in and out all day long, cycling between the Rectory and the streets where he knew every house. Gifts passed through his hands: the wine merchant who lived to be a hundred and was never seen without a flower in his button-hole sent a cheque every year, the old friend in the West Riding put on the railway a bale of cloth from his finishing mill. It contained 'dress lengths'; the Rectory people were to choose first and then dispense the rest. Many a proud household would accept a piece of good Yorkshire cloth when an offer of money would have been impossible.

My father had the immense advantage of having been poor himself all his life. He understood his people, without superiority or sentimentality. He knew what could and could not be done with the means at their disposal. His ready compassion had to make its peace with his sense of probity. How well I remember a visit to Paris, the family's first Continental holiday, when on looking out over the city from the Sacré Coeur, he had been approached by a beggar with a child in arms, and the child held out its little hand as it had been taught to do. My father turned away in anger, furious at the idea of using a child for that purpose. But in the night he had one of those attacks of conscience my mother knew only too well. Next day we were leaving, there was a train to catch, but we sped across Paris in a wildly expensive taxi, up to the Sacré Coeur — but beggar and child were nowhere to be seen.

We were poor by the world's standards, but as children we did not know it; we seemed to ourselves greatly privileged. Certainly we never lacked for small delights. Christmas had always brought presents and these were things that currently we coveted. Not now the appealing stuffed dog or the bow-and-arrows on a card of younger days, but books, pens and satchels; for John, records for the old gramophone or music scores. My parents never gave each other presents; my father would bring home a pot plant for mother — that was all. For years for the two of us there had been stockings at the bedfoot, and even now the same secrecy was involved. That bow-and-arrows on its card which I had seen in a shop window at eight years old and pointed out with transparent nonchalance had been hidden in the dark little closet with the serving hatch, between the study and the butler's pantry, which served my father to hang his cassock and Inverness cape. I found the parcel there quite six weeks before Christmas and used to go and gloat over it sometimes, but never, either before or after it was presented, did I breathe a word about my discovery. Secrecy was *de rigueur*.

The presents were piled up at each end of the dining-room sofa, John's on the left, mine on the right. In earlier days when I did not go with the others to early Communion, there had been a half hour of endurance when I could see the intriguing brown paper shapes but would never have thought of touching them till the others came home.

There was no Christmas tree; and the decorations in the house depended a little on the behaviour of the holly-tree at the garden gate. But one thing had to be bought: the mistletoe. Every Christmas Eve the old branch of mistletoe which had hung in the hall for twelve months was brought in and ceremonially burnt in the fire by my father. It was as much a fixture in the calendar as first-footing. We all stood round watching the flames lick among the dry twigs, while he would say soberly: 'Well, there goes the year. It was a good year for us, thanks be.' Then the new piece would take its place dangling from the banisters.

The magic of Christmas morning: getting up in the dark, walking the mile to church through silent streets, under the little Bar in the Wall which was the entrance to the parish, through the iron gate between old railings and up the avenue of limes with their skeleton boughs meeting overhead, past the strange niches of the Norman porch and into the brightly-lit church with the organ playing, and the greenery masking pitchpine, plaster and stone, turning the church into a memory of woodland...

Wave ye the wreath unfading,
The fir-tree and the pine...

Presents came next, in the warm atmosphere of home. Then another service, and then Christmas dinner. It was late for our usual timetable, because the Rector was chaplain to the workhouse and he went there first, to be present with the Master and the local dignitaries who opened the feast. Meanwhile the rest of the family went home to put the last touches to the festive meal. It was always sizzlingly ready, but on one occasion we were met at the door by Grandma, puzzled and rather scared, saying, 'I suppose there *is* a Christmas dinner, but I can't find it anywhere!'

Mother laughed and opened the door of the big old washing copper built into a corner of the kitchen. It had not been used for washing for many years, but she had installed there a gas stove recently picked up second-hand from the dealer just inside the Bar. Because the smells of turkey and plum-pudding had vanished up the chimney it was no wonder that Grandma, getting up late at her leisure, had been unable to find the cooking.

Grandma. That enigmatic figure was part of all the Christmases I could remember. In August too she always spent a month at the Rectory. She arrived in a cab from the station — and there was always a change in the atmosphere, impossible to ignore but not easy for a child to understand. She was small, neat and spare, with grey hair in smooth bands and sharp little features, grey eyes looking critically through pince-nez, her grey beaded bag containing crochet-work hanging on her wrist, her dress tidy and immaculate. She had just passed her seventieth birthday.

At the beginning of her visit one was on one's best behaviour and any lapses were sure to meet sharp correction, but this was accepted as normal in childhood. It was only gradually that it struck one that the parents were different when she was there; that Mother was anxious, placatory; while Daddy was given to sitting silent at mealtimes, hardly ever addressing a word to Grandma. There was a mystery here.

In the parish, Christmas had a village simplicity. At Evensong for many Sundays, or so it seemed, the Rector would rise from his knees after the prayers, take up the familiar carol sheet and say with satisfaction:

'Now we'll sing carols. We'll start with number twelve, and we'll sing them sitting down.'

So they sat and sang at their ease, the people in the old black pews and the Rector sitting sideways in his oak stall. Carol followed carol, sometimes with a boy taking the page's part in *Good King Wenceslas* to the Rector's beautiful tenor as the King. It was the traditional and naïve ones that he preferred and it would have been impossible to leave out *The First Nowell* or *While Shepherds watched*. He had his own favourites like *I saw three ships come sailing in*, or *When Christ was born of Mary free/In Bethlehem that fair citie*. There were no interspersed readings, nothing carefully rehearsed; it was like a family sing-song.

Looking back, one can see how this would melt away the space between the centuries; no wonder I felt at home in the past. This simplicity had two values for my father: it linked us with old times and it grew out of his deep respect for the simple and poor. It is tempting to think that mediaeval parishioners, if they had come into our home, would have felt *at home*. But of course this could not have been true; they would have found a great deal missing, the Reformation having swept away their landmarks. Eighteenth and nineteenth century people would have been more at sea for a different reason: no hierarchy of class distinction was apparent with us and this would no doubt have been shocking. However, perhaps the congregation which listened to John Wesley preaching one of his last sermons there would have been pleased. But the point in the past where we could have mingled with the old congregation and except for our clothing gone unremarked would perhaps have been in the last year of Edward VI, when the second Prayer-book was new. At that time the rural simplicity in the town, close to the mediaeval spirit but sharing in the new plainness, yet without the constraint of Puritanism, might have hit the same note as church-going in my childhood.

There was a harmony, a oneness, about all the activities of home. On winter evenings in the dusk I would sit in the square bay window at the Rectory — the window which had once had small blue panes in the corners, but now held yellow ones because the Rector liked sunshine — and I would look out into the tiny front garden with its rowan tree and into the darkening road, or back into the room where firelight leapt and danced on the heavily-patterned wallpaper, the solid old table and gleaming brass candlesticks.

From the next room might come the sound of my brother playing the piano. He played well, dreamily or with cascades of flying sound, and his touch was all his own because he was largely self-taught. He loved the music which was modern then and his puzzled elders, brought up on Handel, shook their heads as they heard him playing Debussy; or it might be Rachmaninoff, Grieg or Ravel, or a composer little heard of now, Chaminade. His music had a particular appeal for me, whose fingers were all thumbs — my music lessons had been discontinued. John's music was enough — it spun a web of beauty round everyday life and sometimes I felt eternity there, as if there could be no change: there would always be firelight, the loved faces, the surge of music, the continuity of home.

This would prove to be an enormous asset in the world of the future. However, at the emergent point of childhood it perhaps contributed to making relations with other people more difficult, in that it added to the feeling of being cut off from contemporaries because they were unnecessary.

And there were other isolating facts of which I was unaware. For instance, there was perhaps a special-case feeling about my father's history, that climb from the West Riding cottage and the woollen mill to the University, to modest ideas of scholarship, to priest's orders and a dedicated life. I was always proud of this journey. I did not think of it exactly as a social climb (the atmosphere was too unworldly for that) but as a march towards the best. But in a cathedral town in the early years of the century the parson had a social status which made it unusual for him to have fought his way.

I was beginning to see how my father differed from most clergymen I knew. He had kept his northern accent which was not broad Yorkshire (except when he told stories) but something more subtle, perhaps running back to the Cumberland coast where his mother had been born; when he spoke the liturgy he had no accent. His handwriting was cultured and beautiful, his written English style polished and charming. His speech had an archaic flavour because it was permeated by the Bible. For example, he would say 'nigh unto' for near, 'anon' for soon, 'oftentimes' and 'think you?' and had many other old turns of phrase. He had of course used 'thee' and 'thou' in his youth and the stories of his boyhood still kept them, those tales of practical jokes among the cottages of Bradford which he still remembered with amusement.

He had practical skills which were rare among parsons. My mother told me of a day when they were walking in Wales and stopped to look over a farm gate. In the yard was a man folding fleeces. He looked up at them and said jokingly, 'I'll bet you couldn't do this!' 'Oh, couldn't I?' retorted the parson, vaulting over the gate and settling down to the job as to the manner born.

As in all families, there were mythological tales, often retold with unfailing pleasure. I have always thought kindly of one bit of our family folklore: my father had been curate to a much-loved vicar who left his parish in the south of Yorkshire to become vicar of Middlesbrough on the condition that his curate would go with him. Some years after, there was a Visitation by the new Archbishop of York, Cosmo Gordon Lang. Talk was buzzing in the vicarage drawing-room when someone in the group round the fire urged, 'Give it a poke, man — you've known him seven years!' The Archbishop turned round and saw the curate. '*Have* you known the Vicar seven years?' he demanded to know. My father explained his long connection. And was presented to the first living which fell in the Archbishop's gift.

Most of these stories came out of a remoter past; our parents were Victorians. After all, the first year of their marriage was the last year of the Good Queen. Literary and social historians are prone to ignore the formidable overlap which binds together the generations, or which certainly did so in homes like ours at the beginning of the century.

For example, when I was a child my father wore his top hat on Sundays, though it was becoming old-fashioned to do so. In answer to the amused queries of the young he said, 'I do it to remind people it's Sunday!'

At parties in that gaunt Parish Room which he had so joyfully acquired after manful money-raising efforts, I often danced the polka with him; he was very good at the polka and indeed through my parents I glimpsed a cheerful world of glee-clubs, walking-tours, painting expeditions, invitations to breakfast...Of course all this social intercourse included well-known rules of etiquette about visiting cards, and accepted social forms and ways of meeting people. There seemed to be nothing like this in the world where I was growing up.

'Tell me how you met Daddy,' I would say, and my mother would turn round the wooden 'mushroom' in the heel of the sock she was expertly darning, and recollect a distant summer and a simple tale.

'I was staying at Grassington with your Auntie Sarah,' she would begin...and the rosy, laughing face of 'Auntie' Sarah (no relation, of course, but my godmother) would rise up before me. I knew her only as a plump, lovable, deliciously funny lady who, early-widowed, lived in modest semi-detached luxury in Bradford. Her house seemed palatial to me because it had soft carpets and huge oil-paintings and a conservatory with passion-flowers in it. (Dear Auntie Sarah, kindness itself, tolerance itself...I can remember now the twinkle in her eye and the mock-shocked pulling in of the lip as she told my mother of the escapades of some black sheep or other. She and her quiet elder sister were pillars of the Methodist chapel, and anyone less sanctimonious I have never met.) But that walk in Grassington was long ago, when she and my mother were both twenty. I tried to imagine them: Sarah would be rosy and comical, no doubt, my mother would be as she was in early photographs, a girl with a heart-shaped face, dark appealing eyes and a fringe — though what the photographs did not show was the colour of her golden hair.

On that day in Grassington they had gone out and been drenched in a storm. Running to the inn for shelter, they found there two young men who had been caught in the rain too, and had had to borrow clothes from the landlord until their own were dry. A trap was brought to take them all to the station, to catch trains in different directions, and the innkeeper lent them a huge gig umbrella which my mother held. As they reached the station the young men jumped down, and one of them looked up at the golden girl, to whom he had not spoken a word, and said' 'Goodbye, umbrella!' That was the magic sesame. Months later, the girls were at a concert. Sarah asked, 'Who's that young man who keeps walking up and down and looking at you?' And my mother exclaimed, 'Why, of course, it's *Goodbye, umbrella!*'

Vaguely the courtship and long engagement sketched itself to me — tilted straw hats, high lace collars, leg-of-mutton sleeves, swinging capes and sweeping skirts; drooping moustaches, formal coats and tall collars, walking-sticks, Valentines, volumes of poetry with tender dedications, long absences, grudging permission of a disapproving mamma.

'He wrote beautiful letters,' remembered my mother. 'I used to think they were nicer than he was!' But his optimism and perseverance had swept all obstacles out of the way.

Through these memories came the aroma of Victorianism, its earnestness and idealism, its certainties and reservations. Some things were never mentioned and might just as well never have existed. Sentiment existed — Mother loved it and he derided, being fundamentally the sentimental one of the two. But passion? Darkness? The Victorians knew all about that too, but it had not yet become the fashion to *talk* about it. That would have seemed to them like the exposure of the pale forked roots of a plant. Their Household Words were of a different sort.

DESCRIPTION OF A GARDEN

The night had fallen on a Moorish town,
And in its deep mysterious heart there lay
A Moorish garden, flagged with pave-stones grey,
And lying deep in Shadow.   There did frown
Dark cypress-trees; the moonlight, slanting down,
Glanced on the mystic spire of silver spray
Leaping upon its endless changeful way
Above the dreaming fount.   The dark did drown,
Save for their gleam of marble through the night,
The dim arcades around; and o'er them clung
Wistaria in pale festoons.   The light,
Pale as a ghost's white hand, one long beam flung
Across the square; the magic silence hung
O'er all, and dreamt around the crescent white.

Margaret Mann (aged 14½)
(*Prize-Winner*)

A GREEK LAMENT

Across our Grecian hills the moon has trod,
Arising with her halo and her mist,
And trailing from the hills sea-girt, wind-kissed,
A path of glory to the feet of God.

A few hours more, and o'er the western sphere
Dropping her silver riches spectre-like,
She will have left us, and the cold dawn strike
The quivering stars to silence filled with fear.

Thus also hath the light of wisdom left
Our fated shores, that were of old her grace,
Shedding her glory on the western race—
And all our ancient fame and pride are dead.

M. Mann

Poems by Margaret Mann (Phillips) taken from the school magazine, the *Chronicle*, 1921.

Chapter Three

Acclimatisation

I

But now it was 1920. We had just passed over the watershed, the Kaiser's War, the Great War. But we were not aware yet of the gulf it had fixed between all that older world and the restless twentieth century.

Back at school for a second term, I found things were beginning to move. The initial distrust arising from the opening shock was rapidly modified — if not ever entirely dispelled — by repeated contacts with people.

Evidence of this is supplied by two diary entries in a new notebook, pompously headed *Private Year Book*. The first of these is dated November 11th, 1919, Armistice Day:

> *Memorabilia.*
> *They laughed at my face. Of course they didn't blandly tell me so, but they let me know it right enough. X and Y and Z did it. I said to myself, afterwards, that, if they had told me in words, I should have liked to have said to them, 'Very well. In two years' time let us turn back metally — you will easily remember the day — let us turn back, and see what you have done with your blue eyes and straight noses, and what I have done with other things.' So I am going to keep the record. I used to hope great things of myself. Can I fulfil them?*

Two years was obviously as far as I could dream of looking. It was far in the distance. However, after a couple of further entries, the *Private Year Book* is silent until May 1920, when a breezy reference to 'all this rot which I wrote last year' ushers in a new state of things.

Not that ambition was quite dead; there is a confessed desire to 'keep up the destiny business', but also a recognition that 'it's no good being sentimental and getting no good out of life'. The next remark shows a great step taken:

> *... as for X and Y and Z I really don't see why they shouldn't have a bit of fun, even if it is at my own expense.*

It was a rap over the knuckles for the aloof, superior creature of a few months back.

This was indeed, for me, the diary era. Henry Tilney, who professed to be shocked that Catherine Morland kept no journal *(Northanger Abbey)*, would have been quite satisfied with me. At grips with the shattering discovery of how much pesonal relationships with contemporaries could matter to me, and how complicated they could be, I filled page after page and notebook after notebook with attempts to confide and explain the world-shaking events of my first year at school. Diaries like these are often funny, often pathetic in their naïve analysis of unaccustomed states of mind.

So perhaps, looked at from another world, the events which seem so monumental to us, our revolutions and cold wars, may one day dwindle in our eyes to the proportions of a childish game.

In a single-sex school, where leadership is good, principles strong and knowledge of the world small, the inevitable attachments between individuals have a delicate quality. Later, I came to understand quite clearly how this brought out the unequal proportions of masculine and feminine qualities in the personalities I knew. Without a male element present, the male-female in these adolescents was clearer; as if one said they were not girls but *people*.

In the light of this, there was an unspoken set of rules about friendship. I looked at the people whom fate had thrown me with and some of them obviously stood out as admirable ones, whose acquaintance was to be cultivated, but this very pre-eminence made it unlikely that they on their side would want to be friends with me. By accepted law one never angled for friendship, nor betrayed one's longing for it; if one did, like the enchanted castle in a fairy tale it would vanish away. This was the myth of Psyche. I lived in a maze of sensibility, of symbolic acts and dark speeches, meditating on the chance word or look (Did it mean...? Could it be...?) without a glimmer of understanding of the significance of the desperate importance that attached to these things.

Books helped, of course. It was the age of romance, one sacrificed one's feelings unnecessarily *(It is a far, far better thing that I do, than I have ever done...)*, one was oddly shy or unaccountably bold — and both demonstrations looked idiotic in retrospect. One maintained a rigid mask of indifference, or so one thought, when in reality one was perfectly transparent to the idlest beholder.

Would it all have been easier if my new acquaintances had been of both sexes? Possibly. The young friends of John's whom I had known in my earlier childhood had gone away to school or college, and there were no boys in my world. It would be long before life was to assume two faces again, male and female. As it was, a *modus vivendi* which was pretty reasonable had been evolved by the school. Passionate admiration for mistresses or older girls was humorously treated and called 'being cracked'. Sentimentalism was anathema. Comradeships came and went like figures in a ballet. It would be true to say that no breath of scandal, no faintest suggestion of sexual needs, inside or outside our society, ever came within my knowledge while I was at the school. The contrast between this atmosphere and that of present-day youth is breathtaking. Were we inhibited? At any rate the freedom granted by our innocence was sufficient for deep feeling to grow sometimes between us.

No school run by T-squared could fail to recognise self-sacrifice and self-control as the essential means of reaching the aim of education, which was not seen as self-expression, but as service. T-squared was herself in some ways a martinet. All forms of self-indulgence provoked her scorn. I have a vivid memory of hearing her describe a night at the theatre when she watched, unseen, a young member of her staff eating chocolates from a box after choosing them with intense deliberation. 'It was disgusting!' said T-squared. Whether by coincidence or not, the young teacher's stay at the school was short.

T-squared practised what she preached. Every day she was at Communion in the Minster before beginning her day's work. Probably most of the girls did not know this, but they sensed the rule of life behind all she did. In fact she was a Mother Abbess, demanding the same obedience from those under her as she observed herself. There were only a hundred and twenty girls in the school at this time, and she could know them all personally; no doubt their idiosyncrasies and their ambitions were all reflected in her prayers. The girls all feared her at first and perhaps some never penetrated behind her inflexible bearing; but she had a surprising core of humanity. I found out many things about her through knowing her in later life which I would never have suspected at school. She too was developing and learning as we were.

Even at school, however, I was soon less afraid of her. Behind that eagle-nose and pince-nez there was an occasional twinkle. And always there was the direct look which told you that you were important to her. She was astringent in her manner but you conceded that this was because she wanted the best.

So inside this framework of discipline, the life of the emotions assumed the balance of a minuet. In twos and threes, partners drew near to each other and moved away again, concealing jealousy or possessiveness under a show of calm. You carried their books, waited for them to emerge from school, hung on their words and sometimes nobly left your rival in possession of the field. As I wrote apologetically in my diary in that spring when I was fourteen,

> All this seems very trivial, but there is a great force of Nature behind it, impelling me to all I do.

It was the March and April of that year which seemed so full of romantic episodes. Dominating them, as was to be expected, were the two figures which had ushered me into the new life, Winifred and Miss Elmbridge. It might have been supposed that seeing Winifred every day and cycling with her to school would produce a familiar comradeship and exclude hero-worship. But Winifred had her share of that uncomfortable phase. She became for me a perfect example of Stendhal's *crystallisation*. This tall ivory-pale girl with her dark curls and long fingers was for a while the most wonderful person in the world. The clothes she wore out of school, the green hair-ribbon, coat and skirt of Indian red, or blue silk dress, filled me with quite inexplicable admiration. But there was a saving grace — Winifred was amusing. She had a sudden wit, a dry irony, an ebullient sense of humour. Riding to and from school with her was not only a romantic adventure but a good joke, and even the incidental shopping had its moments, remembered for years. The pork pie I was commissioned to take home and lost en route, the tea-cakes which floated out of the bag and were flattened by a passing bus, seemed to us miraculously funny. The day when because of a puncture I was obliged to go to school by tram and Winifred also came by tram too was a red-letter day specially mentioned in the diary.

Other people liked Winifred too. Of all the Fourth Form there were two whose friendship I coveted, Olive and Beatrice, and the latter was also an admirer of Winifred. She was a firmly-built, rather stocky girl with chestnut hair and one of those fine straight noses which were my secret despair, though she had not been one of the mockers of the *Private Year Book*. Beatrice was a little older than I was and much more mature. In those days I was wildly jealous of her because she was so obviously a far more interesting companion than myself. Beatrice had charm, which she knew how to use, and a wonderful smile. I was watchful and saw her superiority very clearly.

Olive cared for none of these things. She was a tall, lean girl with decided features, a pleasantly curling lip and a caustic power of comment. She had the magnetism of leadership, and a solid straight dependability which drew other people to her. Olive was like a rock. She had not the least coquettishness, no wiles, and when she suspected these in others her judgement expressed itself in a brief sardonic phrase. She was the staunchest and most trusted friend. These two were prominent in my little society and seemed to me important people; were they not top of the examination lists too? It was a leap of ambition to hope that I might be accepted one day as their equal.

And Miss Elmbridge? She was not one of the popular mistresses. I wonder if she ever enjoyed teaching a class. My acquaintance with her gave me inside knowledge and I loved her. With schoolgirls there is rarely a middle opinion; the teacher is too important for that — she must be either despised as negligible or revered as a cult object. Miss Elmbridge was in the former category for most of the school but in the other for me and also for a few of the more perspicacious ones. It is curious to remember, and perhaps impossible to entirely recall, what laceration of feelings or painful raptures can exist under the plump, rather spotty exterior of a Fourth Form child — unless, of course, one has kept the diaries.

I am glad to say that these, though so detailed that they resemble work with a microscope, were not always mawkish. They did occasionally laugh at themselves. I find the following:

> Winifred and Miss Elmbridge are my two goddesses. Miss Elmbridge is very nice to me. I gave her a French poem beginning
> *En avant!*
> *Ma patrie m'invita chez elle,*
> and she has been rather gloomy today.

The dear lady probably had more insight than I credited her with. She probably cottoned on to something when she saw the same candidate come round a second time for an affectionate goodbye at the end of term, for all the world like our friend Dopey. Or when she picked up my French grammar in class and saw her own initials and other graffiti in it. On that occasion she remarked, 'It seems to be a very *commentative* sort of book — perhaps I had better not look at it any more...' Then there was the time when she spent half an hour after class talking to me about *education;* her own comment, on leaving, was that 'she didn't know why she had spent so long talking nonsense'. Looked at from long afterwards, this sounds like a person who, feeling herself to be unusually significant in a young life, had been moved to express some of her own ideals. But the diary does not say what they were.

A dawn of trust shows in the diaries. Apart from that initial cold douche, there was no unkindness to relate, only gaucheries, unexplained longings, failures and withdrawals, and conversations whose promise of happiness could hardly be believed. People were mysterious, and my own inner world most of all, in its richness and its desires. As my diary stated,

> I can't understand myself. I wish I could — it would really be twice as convenient!

II

This new sensitivity did not divert all my attention from the outside world, nor mask the joys of spring. As the days lengthened, the dash on flying wheels through the town became more light-hearted. Past the War Office I

Rear view showing the 'new' hall (1921).

York College Junior School.

went, the old Empire music-hall which had become a roller skating rink and then a cinema, and so down the hill from which one could see the long grey outline of the Minster over the crowding roofs, and on by streets sometimes uninterestingly new but more often narrow and mediaeval, with plaster fronts and overhanging gables, to arrive at last at Minster Gate.

Much of the school life was passed in and around the Minster. That spring a confirmation service was held in the Lady Chapel, beneath the huge hanging curtain of many-coloured glass that was the East Window. In fact, I was to sit under it many times, till it became quite natural to pick out the creation of sun and moon, the making of birds and fishes, the garden of Eden with its golden fruit, and Adam and Eve on each side of the tree; or lower down, angels with trumpets from the Book of Revelation, and cities with cobalt skies behind them. The chief impression at this time was the extraordinary difficulty of singing in that space between the bases of enormous pillars and that high faraway roof. One's voice seemed a mere tiny piping lost in the air. I remember my eyes would turn to where Winifred and Beatrice stood sharing a hymn book and Beatrice would catch my jealous glance.

School occasions were few. The most important was the prize-giving and I had been a spectator of that in my first term. As the school had no assembly hall yet, the ceremony was held in the beautiful ancient building round the corner. This inspired some awe because it was used for gatherings of a clerical kind. It was a magnificent dusky place, perfect in its timbered gables collected round a pebbled courtyard, and inside it was all heavy oak beams and dark wainscot and portraits of departed worthies. One of these portraits struck me, I remember, as one of the most saintly faces I had ever seen — it was Archbishop Maclagan. For this occasion the girls wore white dresses, sang songs and received their prizes. I looked on with some surprise and with a little embarrassment too because no one in the audience could be expected to know why I hadn't got a prize. But there was consolation in a smile from Mother and a wink from Daddy, and fascination at the sight of Miss Elmbridge who had for once got out of the grey cardigan and into a green dress and an academic gown, mysteriously bordered with shot silk. When I told her afterwards that she ought to wear it in school, she mischievously chose to read *Le Corbeau et le Renard*, twinkling at me over the Fox's flattery.

There was one occasion in the town which was also an occasion for the school — the Annual Gala (pronounced *gayler* by the plebs and *garler* by the nobs). It was held in a large field close to the railway, and united all the town in three days of simple enjoyment. First there was the dim, rarefied pleasure of the flower show: walking through the cool marquees with their scent of damp moss and roses, to admire the prize blooms and cloudy bouquets and little landscape gardens. This was solemn and rather like being in church.

One emerged from the flower tent to blink into the glare of June sunshine and find all the amusement of a fair: roundabouts, bearded ladies, fortune-tellers, acrobats on a stage, coconut shies and try-your-strength. Sometimes there was the extra joy of a balloon ascent. In the evening fireworks and flares lit up the row of great chestnut trees on the edge of the field. At the very end of this open space stood a mental hospital and I often looked at it with solemn speculation and wondered whether the patients minded. Were they frightened by the fireworks and worried by the hoarse tunes of the roundabouts, or glad to have the fun of the fair brought close to them? Or maybe saddened to see the normal world come so near?

In June 1920 the diary was busy with the Gala:

> *Winifred is not coming to the Gala this afternoon — it is too bad. I'm frantically disappointed, and so is she. There is going to be a missionary service or something in the Minster, I believe — and the Archbishop forgot it was the Gala, so he's frightened that there'll be no one there, and Miss Tarrant came and asked the Sixth to go, and Winifred volunteered, but Cherry said she was going to the Gala. That's their characters.*

This seems to show that hero-worship was seeking a rational basis. It also throws a rather unflattering light on the lordly figure of Cosmo, the Archbishop whom I so greatly admired. The following day, however, there were no missionary services and the long evening after school was spent happily among the fair lights, accepting with ecstasy Winifred's invitation to 'go down the mat', holding her hand tightly among the shoving crowd and riding to victory and triumph over their heads on the shiny-necked wooden horses.

The City was the world. Everything else was far away. The War was over. I looked very little at newspapers, which seemed to be a man's privilege. My father read them and it looked odd to see my mother doing so — an impression which died hard.

If I had read them then, I might have seen the headline: *The most awful spectacle in history, millions of children naked and starving in Europe,* with the agonized plea of the Save the Children Fund. What I did note was the expression on my godmother's plump rosy face when she said in her comfortable West Riding manner, 'They came round collecting, and there was a picture of a little child right *pined*'.

Hardship showed in other ways and the top drawer in the study was always full of pennies, to be handed out at the door in small handfuls to wandering men in search of the price of a bed. My father had his own decided views on mendicancy. 'They wouldn't be asking for it if they didn't need it,' he would say. Knowing he could not give much, his system was to give a little to all, and, if it became blatantly clear that the hard-luck story was a plain fraud, this was just the luck of the game. His door was well-known, it seemed, to all the men who tramped the main road from the south. Sometimes I had to go and wash off their chalked messages to each other on the gateposts.

Just occasionally he reacted in sharp self-defence. One day a particularly plausible tramp went away with half-a-crown, a large subsidy for those days, and he had barely left the front steps when his benefactor was assailed by doubt. The Rector slipped out and saw the man turn straight into the nearest public-house, the *Light Horseman*. To think of his scanty means being immediately drunk off was too much, so he followed and arrived at the bar just as his half-crown had been plonked down for a foaming pint. Picking up the coin he pocketed it, saying 'Thank you, that's mine.' The cream of the story was that one of the witnesses standing by was gamekeeper to a local lord who had just been approached for help with the purchase of the Parish Room. The man told his master the story as a good joke, and the noble earl was so tickled by the parson's canny behaviour that he sent a large donation.

Social questions had no place in the diary, but one event almost set its pages on fire: the visit of Sir John Martin Harvey in *Hamlet*

It was a first experience of great acting. Although I realised he was too old for the part, this rather added to than detracted from my admiration. He had dignity, a spare handsomeness and above all consummate experience. In spite of the fact that I had read a good deal of Shakespeare, mostly comedy, I had never actually seen a play acted. The impact of *Hamlet* was immense. I was entranced from the unfolding of the first scenes by the stunned recognition that so much of the dialogue was familiar; to an English ear it is like taking over an inheritance. I exhausted my adjectives in trying to describe the effect of *A little more than kin and less than kind*, or *Angels and ministers of grace defend us!* I was in the glorious state where nothing can be a cliché. The actor enthralled me. 'I shall always remember him,' I wrote. And it was true. Even the diary's clumsy unpractised account reveals the variety and subtle shading of that finished performance.

> *Then Act II, Scene 2 was splendid — how Hamlet comes in reading, and Polonius talks to him — there was a couch on the stage, and it was lovely to see him throw himself on it, and put his feet up, or one foot. And in the same scene where he speaks of 'man' it was glorious, with that little smile about his mouth which did not lose its sadness, I think, except then. And when he spoke to Ophelia in Act III.2, the words look rough written, but when he spoke them his voice was, oh, so tender! And you knew that he really did love her, and was voluntarily giving her up. And then at the play, he is so bitterly, dramatically gay, and lies at Ophelia's feet. Then when he speaks to his mother, and then — 'Do you not come your tardy son to chide?' And his unselfish sorrow as he says, 'Assume a virtue, if you have it not'.*

And at the very end, how the audience strained to catch his last words — 'The rest is silence!' And they wouldn't let him go — he came back again and again with their clapping, keeping up his character to the end, not even smiling till the fourth or fifth time he was recalled. Every time the curtain went up he was walking leisurely off the stage, and had to come back again, and bow, still in the black doublet and trunk hose and fur collar of Hamlet. At last he had to speak, and said that he thanked the audience for their understanding reception of the performance, and bowed again, with that little smile on his lips, I think — and then they let him go.

Sir John must have been contented with his provincial audience that evening. Certainly, for one child there it was an introduction to a new world.

III

Perhaps this is the place to say something about the poetic imagination — and to analyse the influence of poetry as a dynamic in my life.

Poetry had seemed to me the most important thing in life since I was eight years old. At first I supposed this was the case with everybody. The grown-ups who were so serious over trifles I presumed had all started that way, with the voice calling them and their election clear. But they had turned away from the commands of that voice and chosen to live in the plains rather than on the mountains. Somewhere, obviously, there were grown-ups who had not done this. But it did not need Wordsworth to tell me that 'the light of common day' had been the element that conquered in the lives of most people.

Growing a little older, I began to perceive, or think I perceived, that this assumption was not always true. People lived, it seemed, more comfortably than I had thought possible in the *un*poetic world, without any sense of guilt about abandoning their calling. Then was my own experience peculiar? This question was too difficult to decide: *yes* would mean conceit, *no* would mean there were circumstances I had not understood. I soon ceased to worry about this. For myself, the sense of calling was a dominant note.

However, it is vital to remember that this sense was accompanied by much diffidence, which never quite drowned it. Of course, one ought not to consider oneself marked out. And one must remember that one was a girl. A jeering voice said, *Women don't do these things. If they aspire to such heights, they are deceiving themselves. Take yourself seriously and you will be a fool.* But I never quite believed that voice. I heard it in later years in the mouth of a psychologist who said to me, 'Women don't create.' It was easy to respond by asking him if he had read *Wuthering Heights* (the answer was 'No').

But at fourteen logical argument was not the compelling force: and what made me go on writing verse was the sheer importance of the experience itself. It was the continuous preoccupation of my adolescence. What I wanted was not only to produce the finished poem — which anyway always looked different next day, rather as a beautiful pebble loses its gleam when taken out of the water — but to experience the most precious thing, the processs itself. The ideas which shaped themselves into poetry apparently came from beyond, through a door in the mind one did one's best to keep ajar: on the other side of that there was some unfathomable sea. After the first shock of recognition, which usually came from the perception of some special kind of beauty, and later from the relating of an experience of one's own to something universal, there was the longer work of shaping. Experience taught me that the right word always existed, even under the restriction of rhyme-schemes. The business was to find it. Nothing in life gave quite the same thrill as the obedient homing of a word, like a carrier pigeon, to the unfinished line, and the longer one had despaired of it the more welcome it was.

The products were juvenile. But I had no doubt that what was happening to me, as I went through the creative process, was what happened to the great poets. The difference in outcome was obvious, but it was one of degree and not of kind.

So when other people were developing more concrete and more easily realisable ambitions, I kept in sight the star of poetry and made it my intangible but imperious aim. I knew it would be regarded as wildly presumptuous so must be kept as secret as possible. Only one person knew the force of it: Mother, who, at the hearth, was the all-seeing critic.

IV

The examinations at the end of the spring term revealed that it was possible to have another ambition, that of getting one's name high on the lists which began to appear on the classroom notice-board, if possible in red (over 75%). Olive, Beatrice and I were rivals in some spheres and it was a great day for schoolgirl pride when Beatrice came tearing into the cloakroom where I was battling with a tangled shoelace and cried, 'Shake — we've tied in French!'

T-squared, however, summoned me to an interview. The diary describes this minutely. Again she reminds me of a Mother Abbess interviewing the youngest novice. She had evidently studied those class-lists with close attention.

She began by remarking that she thought I had not worked as hard at

Prayer-book study and arithmetic (both subjects taught by herself) as I had at some other things. Did *I* think I had?

All I could say was, 'I don't know.'

She at once wanted to know whether I did not think over all my day at night. This was a novel idea. I did not know that what was being suggested to me was an *examen de conscience*, a principle going back through the mediaeval church to the precepts of Pythagoras. I simply told the truth.

'No, I don't.'

'You ought to,' replied T-squared seriously, 'then you would not have had to tell me that you didn't know whether you had worked or not.

She tapped the desk with her pencil meditatively, then continued. Perhaps, she said, I might think she was rather fussy about the method of setting sums down. But her girls had always been noted for their excellent way of doing this. If one got six marks for a sum, it was three for the answer and three for the way the sum was put down. So much, at any rate, the diary recorded; it was the measure of what I had understood. Then a slight misunderstanding occurred.

'Isn't there a feeling at the bottom of your heart —' T-squared paused.

Ever willing to oblige, I filled in anxiously, 'Yes..'

But she finished, '...that I'm really rather fussy about this?'

Here was a poser! I said nothing: there seemed to be nothing to say. T-squared took up her parable again. If I could do well in English and French, I ought to try all the harder with the things I couldn't do.

She was really trying to get down to my level, to help me. Standing by that desk in the severe little room, I listened. It got through to me that she was not angry. The silly little misunderstanding had broken the stiffness of the interview and for the first time I felt a real person before the gaze of T-squared. I found a voice and a straight look.

Trying to analyse the degrees of neglect, I told her that I had perhaps worked less hard at the Prayer-book, but I *had* worked at arithmetic. T-squared smiled. I assumed it was because she liked boldness (*'She liked that,'* said the diary. *'She loves you to answer back and show her that you aren't afraid of her.'*) It was too much to expect, perhaps, that I should understand the watchful care she exercised and the pleasure it gave her to achieve a degree of communication. But I took the hand she gave me as she wished me a happy holiday. I turned to leave, then some inkling must have come to me of what it was all about, causing me to hesitate with my hand on the door-knob. The diary recorded, *I didn't want her to think her niceness was wasted, so I turned at the door and said 'Thank you very much, Miss Ellett.'* She gave a motion of her head and I went out.

Oh, small school! Watchful Head! Uniqueness accorded to the slightest burgeoning of personality — how precious it all was!

V

However, this caution was all very well. Term began again on the fifth of May. There had never been a spring like this one. And in the heady spring days I threw reason to the winds and ambition suffered a severe setback.

On the 22nd May I went to fetch the butter from the grocer's; he had moved from the old shop in the parish to another in a better district. Because he was still churchwarden and his faithful help during the lean years of war was not to be forgotten, we made the longer journey. On the way I was passed by a car decked with white ribbons. Peering inquisitively in, I saw the bride lean forward with the white veil on her hair to speak to the young man at her side. ...*in the full rigout of a story wedding*, I recorded, adding *Good gracious, if it ever comes to my turn, won't I do things properly!*

Romance was only accidentally connected with weddings; there was plenty of it everywhere that May. It was so extraordinary to me to have relationships at all; to glimpse the possibility of being a person among people. Winifred might be still on her pedestal, but others were coming closer, the impalpable fog was thinning.

Youthful conversations seemed to hold immense significance. One day I came out of school with Beatrice, who was looking ruefully at her flat tyre. We stood at the gate opposite the Minster, waiting for Olive to emerge. Our conversation was momentous to me.

>Beatrice You and Olive seem to be very pally just now.
>(This was an unprecedented attack on privacy and amazed me.)
>Self [Awkwardly] Yes. [Pause] It's the bane of my life.
>Beatrice What is?
>Self Trying to make people see I want to be pally.
>Beatrice Did *you* want to be?
>Self [Elusively] I want to be pally with everyone, more or less.
>Beatrice Like me, so do I.
>Self [Humbly] Well, everybody likes you.
>Beatrice [Laughing] No one dislikes me, and no one dislikes you.
>(Decidedly something was happening!)

Olive had succeeded in disentangling her bicycle from the heap, and the next thing was to cope with Beatrice's flat tyre. How was she to get as far as the games field? With new confidence I ran to a man's bicycle propped up on the Minster railings, detached the pump and took it over to Beatrice.

'Don't,' they said. 'He'll think you're stealing.'

But the tyre was pumped up and the pump replaced in a moment, and we were all off down the road with the wind in our plaits.

Why did this tiny scene of the pump have such significance? Later on, I thought I understood. But at the time it was just delightful to be one of them, even to be able to raise a laugh, to be listened to, to be someone.

It went right to my head. The girls watched the transformation with interest and the staff with disapproval. The quiet little swot had turned into the noisiest, silliest, most harebrained member of the class.

Through the long days of June, in the cool dark classroom or out in the sunshine of the crowded garden, or sitting in the shade of trees on the edge of the playing fields watching tennis finals, I was in swinging high spirits, accepting and accepted, surprising the others by my gusto, and surprised myself to find out how friendly they were.

At the school sports, I watched Olive in a mighty tussle with another competitor in the bicycle tortoise race. The aim was to be last, and Olive was ahead of the other girl for two-thirds of the course, and then she stopped dead. This brought the other bicycle level with her, a few yards from the tape, and I burned with admiration and pride as Olive edged forward coolly and won by three inches. It was a victory which summed up what I admired in Olive, her tenacity and control; qualities of maturity and balance which I felt the need of in myself.

On the 18th June Beatrice and I went to play tennis and were prevented by a violent storm. This gave us a happy afternoon in the pavilion, where we found a store of buns, coconuts and lemonade, and the sentimental musings we exchanged were duly recorded in the diary. The uncertainty of the heart filled burning pages in which dramatic passages on renunciation alternated with naïve speculations on whether the rival admirer would 'give in first'. All was completely decorous, and the development of emotion was partnered by practice in the art of words. Mercifully no one but the writer was ever to read them. For once, a notebook was completed, and ended in a more rational state of equilibrium:

> *Well, I've come to the end of my book. God bless us all, and help us to do our work well, and help me to be a poet, and make the ones I love love me.*

But in July Nemesis struck. The first blow was the news that Miss Elmbridge was leaving.

> *Whatever shall we do? Oh dear, and I'd only just begun to know her — I never shall now — and Winifred, oh, poor Winifred!*

Winifred had known the bad news for a fortnight and had not told anybody. It came to me in the end from Beatrice, through a note passed in a lesson. I sat there stupefied. Miss Elmbridge going to another school! And *Winifred* leaving the Sixth to start a training! My interesting world came crashing about my ears. Without these people life would come to a stop.

The examination lists went up. I was nowhere near the top. No red-letter mentions for me this time. Other girls whom I had not thought of as rivals had been working steadily and had outpaced me. I thought bitterly of the wasted time, and of the last term fizzling out, shorn of its jest and repartee. Miss Steele summoned me and asked sternly why I had failed geography. In vain I pleaded that the subject was new to me, and I was completely floored by questions about Ireland. 'You should have known enough to get more than twenty-four per cent,' she told me severely. Oddly enough, one of my consolations was to collect suitable Latin proverbs to meet the emergency. *Post tenebras lux* was cheering, and so was *Quae nocent, docent*, but *Non sum qualis eram* was only too true.

Why was Miss Elmbridge leaving? A few loyal supporters made urgent enquiries at the end of term.

'Why are you leaving, Miss Elmbridge?'

'Oh, do you want reasons?' said Miss Elmbridge brightly.

'I know, it's *us*.'

'Oh, yes, you in particular!' mocked Miss Elmbridge, crinkling up her eyes at the corners in the way I loved. 'Never mind, I'll come back and see you.'

'I'm giving up French, Miss Elmbridge!'

'Now that *would* be a nice thing for me to find out when I come back...' etc.

There was no help for it. The last day came, the last hour. We sang the end-of-term hymn about ...*those who here shall meet no more*, and I looked into the future and saw a desert without hope, except for a letter from Winifred in the long separation of summer holidays.

VI

It seems curious that holidays should mean separation, not only from Olive and Beatrice, who both lived far away and stayed with relatives during the term, but from Winifred whose house was just across the road. The reason was, no doubt, that our absences were not synchronised. I went to Morecambe to stay with Grandma, and when I came home Winifred had gone to Scotland. The break was endless.

Going to Morecambe had its pleasures, of course. We went by train, starting by London and North-Eastern and changing lines at Leeds, being carried by the Midland line out of Yorkshire, across the backbone of hills: this was called with an odd disregard of war-time terminology 'going over the top'. There had been treasured moments of childhood when Mother chanted to the slow motion of the train chuntering up the eastward slopes '*Think I can, think I can, think I can...think..I...can...*' until quite suddenly the top was reached and the train sped merrily down the other side to delighted shouts of *'Thought I could, thought I could, thought I could!'*

There were lovely small stations on the way with names like Kirkby Stephen and Gargrave, and at Bentham, one of the last stops, John and I — and Mother too — were convulsed by a harassed bucolic man who pushed an immense woman into the compartment with many warnings:

'Look out, Ma, your knitting's trailing, you'll lose the ball under the seat, and then... Don't you drop off now, you'll happen miss our Florrie, and then...'

Morecambe station was different from all others: it was light, airy, clean and had the smell of the sea. The hanging baskets of geraniums gave it a garden look. Suddenly it was good to be there. We stepped out into the unbelievable air and carried our bags to the tram. There it all was, the same place as last year, and yet all to be rediscovered; what had changed was oneself. We rattled along the Promenade and turned inland through narrow streets which were part of the old Morecambe, not far removed from the modest fishing and holiday place Mother had known as a girl. It lay clustered round its parish church, behind its pebbly beach with the panoramic view of all the Lakeland mountains; the view was still there, but a big seaside resort had grown up around the little town and was already threatening to squeeze it out. There were now only corners, the old jetty, the quiet lanes round the church, which told of earlier days.

Still, the place had a vivid life. In the windows of the terraced cottages sat the fishermen's wives, picking shrimps so fast that you could hardly see their fingers move. In the sweetshops there were strange wares shaped like seaside pebbles, or sticks of giant rock with the name running right through, or huge peppermint humbugs. Outside the centre of the town the houses had little gardens in front of them, edged by walls topped with pieces of limestone in grotesque shapes. There was a bridge over the railway line, oddly called York Bridge (perhaps because it was on Lancaster Road?) And there on the outskirts of the town was a row of tall semi-detached pebbledashed houses, with long gardens at the front, long paths running uphill from the solid gateposts, trim grassplots and flowerbeds with few flowers but a lot of the silver leaves I called Donkey's Ears. And at the open door of Long Garth stood... Grandma.

Small and unchanging, dapper and unruffled from the smooth grey plait on the top of her head to her size two shoes, Grandma was a recurrent mystery. Why she should be formidable was not clear, except that she made sharp remarks sometimes, and it was impossible to guess the thoughts behind the rimless pince-nez. Her personality impregnated the house, from the trim little hall with the weatherglass and the grandfather clock to the modest little sitting-room dominated by the dreadful enlargement of John and me as children, and the glass-fronted cupboard housing the Crown Derby china. Most of all, her careful, ambitious spirit was reflected in the front room, little used, where the lace-curtained bay window, the pale green walls and green carpet with its wreath of flowers, and the ornaments in black bog-oak, all basked in the smell of camphor; going in there was like penetrating into a cave under the sea.

I never knew that room to be inhabited. No one ever sat in the green brocade chairs or trod on the immaculate carpet, except for the purpose of dusting the what-not or drawing down the blinds against the sun. All life went on in the sitting-room and its adjacent kitchen.

But behind the house there was a long garden full of strangeness for me. First a small asphalt yard bordered by box hedges and flanked by a great arch of yew, through which the path ran on past a little orchard, grassy under the trees, past a vegetable plot planted with gooseberry bushes to a sunny hedge, against which my father in his courtship days had built a roofed garden-seat, quite quiet and remote. Tall yellow daisies edged this long path, and seemed to collect the light in the evening. Other gardens surrounded this one but there never seemed to be anyone in them; the old man next door was rarely to be seen, and the whole place was curiously quiet.

On the garden-seat in the summer sunshine I sat and meditated about my year of school. It looked like a pattern now. At the time a disconnected jumble, it now lay before me as a connected whole. Like a play, I thought, *with a plot and crises and strange unlooked-for Last Act.* It was a first experience of something which was going to happen often: the events which had seemed such a hotch-potch of fortuitous incidents were really a jigsaw completely interlocking. Often the same earnest contemplation of a part of life lived was to reproduce the same result: the kaleidoscope shifted and showed a design. Would the master-plan come clear in the end? It was this thought which lent excitement to the idea of death.

The family was not complete: Daddy still had to come, on one of his long succession of motor-cycles. No doubt it was cheaper if more laborious. His arrival was a longed-for event, and the shimmering faceted blue of the sea needed him to complete its beauty. When he came, contentment should have been entire.

Yet, on that afternoon when I sat at the table poring over his old Greek grammar (I was to begin Greek next term and the alphabet fascinated me) my absorption must have made me give him a rude answer and this brought a reprimand on my head for impertinence. It came as a small shock for I had no idea that there was any special reason for him to be edgy in Grandma's house. Why should he specially long for attention and deference there? I was hardly equipped to understand either the question or the answer.

For the first time an influence from outside the family was acting on me. Far away there were people who mattered too, and so much. I waited for Winifred's letters and lived with them when they came, long and neatly written and amusing. The sight of the blue envelope was a tonic and it lay in my pocket like a talisman. Beatrice wrote too after a long delay. Olive sent a cheerful card with a view of Whitby. And, wonder of wonders, Miss Elmbridge contributed a postcard of Ypres Town Hall as it had been before the bombing. Where had she got that? I was suspended between the two worlds, impatient to begin the next instalment. *Oh, month, hurry up! Days, fly!* said the diary — and then guiltily contradicted the wish to tamper with Time. The best way to describe the new variable rhythms of life was to use the language of music. I selected terms which fitted the course of that first year: *Adagio* at first, then *Grandioso, Affetuoso* and *Festoso*, but finally, alas, *Doloroso, Affretando*. Language certainly had a spellbinding power over me.

VII

Back home again, I had too much time. Luxuriating in melancholy along Lord Mayor's Walk, where aeons of time ago I had propped myself up on my bicycle to read Rossetti, I decided to call on Miss Elmbridge. There were books to return...anyway. At fourteen the space of a year seems to be far away. One had grown so much since my early visits. It was strange to see the house looking just the same, the bay window, a greengrocer's cart drawn up in front. A noise of hammering came from the regions upstairs. I knocked, and after a long time a voice said, 'Well, she's there. Go up, you know where it is, don't you?'

So I climbed the stairs and arrived flushed and nervous in the room where I had had those first French lessons. In blue overall, Miss Elmbridge was stooping over a packing-case beside an empty bookshelf. She straightened up, saw me, and welcomed me with commendable cordiality — after all, she was in the middle of her packing, and a shy teenager to make conversation with must have been something she could do without. But she was as usual immensely kind, and I felt this as I sat on the edge of my chair looking at the blue envelope from Winifred sticking its corner out of the letter-rack. I listened to Miss Elmbridge's voice talking (as the diary reports), *with a mixture of friendliness and that patronising responsibility which belongs to mistresses only, as a race apart.*

So there I left Miss Elmbridge, whom I never saw again, and turned round to face the future.

York High School pre-1908. The School closed in December 1907 and the York College for Girls opened on 24 January 1908 at 69 Petergate.

York High School pre-1908.

Chapter Four

Breathing-space

I

The new term, when it came a week later, brought changes which plunged me into real depression. It was incredible what a little re-organisation could do to make me feel my life was ruined.

Naturally I had expected Miss Elmbridge's departure and Winifred's changed status — she was now a student teacher in the Kindergarten — to deplete my landscape, but it was the reconstitution of the form which came as a severe blow to my pride. Not only some of the older girls, but Beatrice and another of my contemporaries had gone up into the Fifth. Imagine my humiliation in discovering myself to be still in the Fourth Form — in IVa, it is true — with a rabble of youngsters from Form III..... I felt sure that if I had worked properly in that vanished summer term I too could have 'gone up' with Beatrice, who now had new friends and new work to do. It was true that Olive was still in the Fourth with me, but then Olive was younger than I was. In any case, she was more sensible, and I was leaving her out of account when I wrote fiercely in the diary,

> *The present Fourth! which means the scum of the former Fourth and the 'cream' of the former Third. I feel inclined to swear, and what's more, I indulge at times in that harmless pastime.*

Trivial reasons for adolescent blues? Yet they were important at the time and every change of wind in the realm of feeling in those vital years had a connection with underlying problems and a meaning. It is no exaggeration to say that my life might have been totally different if this small check had not occurred. The only thing to do now was to work. The purpose of this resolution was, I thought, simply in order to regain my self-respect, merely to achieve an out-of-season move into the higher form. But it was more far-reaching than that. I discovered that life presents people with dilemmas. It looked like a choice between work and people, head and heart, ambition and happiness. Childish now, the dilemma would grow into the fundamental question which faces the creative life. Intellectually one recognised that the goal was worth the struggle and firm resolutions were made about single-mindedness and sacrifice. In one's inmost heart one hoped that there would be room for a compromise, an integration. The debate had opened.

How prosaic and dull the days seemed! The coating of magic, the 'crystallisation' had gone. Life had become ordinary. Its ordinariness seemed personified in Miss Elmbridge's young successor, who was kind, interested in my work, *quite nice*. If I had only known it, this year of easy work and gentle progress, this lying fallow, was a breathing-space which T-squared had been far-sighted enough to give me. It was one of the most valuable things I could have had. But years passed before that became apparent.

Emotionally it was a breathing-space too. *My life is devoid of romance*, said the diary. But it also added a query as to whether some people had not been spoken of too often in its pages, perhaps to the point of pall? *Certainly it is a refreshment to speak of somebody else, and rather rejuvenates one: perhaps I had better let them rest for a little.* Love would prosper better, I thought, if left to smoulder; my bulbs would grow better if not perpetually pulled up by the roots.

The term wore on, work was easy, life was calm. From the new form room window we could see the workmen erecting a prefabricated assembly hall, and when the end wall went up we all crowded to the windows. It was to be ready for the prize-giving in December. Simple activities like a missionary play acted by the 'King's Messengers' (junior supporters of the S.P.G.) were added to the curriculum. I felt guilty about being half-hearted about these dramas; they seemed to have so little to do with the real work of Christian effort in heathen lands. But sometimes they struck a deeper note, often in hymns.

> *In concert with the holy dead*
> *The warrior Church rejoices.*

That was as stirring as *'The Saints of God! their labours past'* or the steady vision of

> *The golden evening brightens in the west;*
> *Soon, soon to faithful warriors comes their rest.*

Singing played an appreciable part in school life. The teacher was the sub-organist of the Minster, a tall thin young man with spectacles and a sense of humour. He chose a wide range of songs from the usual school fare... *Where'er you walk, Nymphs and Shepherds, Strawberry Fair, Sir Eglamore*... and sometimes more ambitious ones too, testing out our taste by taking a vote with our eyes shut. A mistress was always in the room; whether from an old Victorian custom, or because we were not trusted to behave decorously with a young man, and an outsider to the school, remains obscure.

It was to him that I owed a small delicious experience that term. One day in late autumn T-squared asked me to take a message to him in the Minster on my way home. I could give the note to one of the vergers, she said. It was already dark when I wheeled my bicycle down the path out of school and propped it against the Minster railings. The familiar place looked different at night, and there was some sense of mystery and importance in pushing open the panel marked CLOSED in the great oak door and stepping inside. The Minster was quite dark, except for a few lights at the entrance to the choir and in the organ-loft. They lit up small areas with a strange reddish glow, and above my head soared the rest of the building, guessed rather than seen. It resembled a primeval forest of springing lines and branching arches receding into shadow. No walls appeared, but here and there the great windows presented blank surfaces, and tiny bits of carving or ironwork caught fractions of light. It was a different place from the Minster I knew. It almost seemed to have stripped off its stone covering and to stand there like a monument of darkness shot through with fire. This intense impression was added to my knowledge of the place as one learns more of a friend in a new and unfamiliar mood.

Struggling to be articulate about the sense of awakening, the diary describes a day when I was walking along the street under the shadow of the dark stone wall which then hemmed in the Castle, in an early evening of November. An old woman was playing a barrel-organ, or as I called it a hurdy-gurdy, in the gutter. Mindful of family custom, I gave her some coppers and turned away to go on towards home. As I went, the hurdy-gurdy struck up a tune which I knew well, a tune which haunted my whole generation. Suddenly I had one of those moments when one becomes utterly conscious. Everything round me, the dark wall which I knew concealed the bright Keep, the faces of the people in the street, the awareness of self, resolved like bits in a kaleidoscope into the realisation of *Now*. I made an effort to express the inexpressible.

> *When the old tune, which was slow, haunting and sweet, came to my ears, suddenly there came one of those glimpses I sometimes get of Life itself — the realisation that I was indeed living in the world of which I had read, that there were things to do and know, that it was not a dream, but that I was I, and Eternity to come! And my soul struggled to free itself; and suddenly it seemed to be halfway out of its prison, up to the fringe — pointing towards another atmosphere of which I knew nothing. I distinctly felt the difference of that region outside the flesh, and I let go of my body and staggered as I walked — and the staggering pulled me back, into it again.*

It was proper to the time that the tune should be the *Destiny Waltz*, but a revealing phrase pointed to the importance of *the world of which I had read*.

That the experience of literature should come first, and that of events second, was a peculiarity due to the long reading hours of my unschooled childhood. The world of the past seemed native, that of the present foreign; was this a disadvantage or a liberation, a stepping back, as it were, to view present reality with a detached eye? No doubt it was both.

II

Occasions of a more active kind reappear like vignettes or pictures on a screen. There was my first real prize-giving, and this time I had a prize, the poetry prize, which had fallen like a ripe plum into my lap for a sonnet about a Moorish garden. Why these gardens should have haunted me so obsessively I cannot say; it was to be over forty years before I actually saw the Alhambra. The garden I saw at fourteen was a paved court, with a central fountain and outlying arcades hung with wistaria, and somewhere in it dark cypresses cut across the slanting moonbeams. My poetic landscapes were nearly always without figures. The prize brought a congratulatory postcard from Miss Elmbridge, which I received with gratitude and surprise.

There was one trouble about the prize-giving. It was preceded by the customary display of pupils' talent, and then T-squared, who was a good hand at publicity where her beloved school was concerned, took it into her head to advertise the fact that we learnt Greek. More accurately, one pupil was learning Greek; for the little sandy-haired Latin mistress (a lover of the classics with a kind heart, though given to quailing before the mob) was now engaged in teaching me the rudiments. (It would have been better if I had taken them more seriously, but I think we proceeded rather too quickly for them to sink in.) On this occasion I found myself condemned to recite, as one of the items in the programme, the prayer of Socrates from Plato, with the help of a Phaedrus in the shape of Beatrice. Socrates had quite a lot to say, while Phaedrus was let off with one remark. In vain I had protested that this level of Greek was far more advanced than anything I could have been expected to reach in under a term, and therefore I felt somewhat dishonest. In any case I thought I would look idiotic standing up in front of my parents and what would seem a vast assembly in my white starched frock and black shoes and stockings with my arms raised in the attitude of an *Orante*. What a fate! But T-squared was adamant; so the passage had to be memorized and spoken.

T-squared was one of that unfairly treated generation of women who had passed examinations but were not allowed academic dress. All the new young teachers who joined her staff came out on prize-giving day in resplendent hoods, but T-squared had to be hoodless in a dignified garment known as a hostess gown, though looking no less a headmistress for that.

Beside her sat the Archbishop. It was quite alarming to see two such presences in juxtaposition. The Archbishop's speech was less formidable than might have been expected. He looked round the new hall and observed that it was useful, unpretentious, spacious and warm and had the most beautiful view of the Minster. And thus he was emboldened to hope that every girl in it would be useful, unpretentious, high-minded, warm-hearted and take a splendid view of life. Partly jocose, partly moralising, his speech sounded over the heads of the girls in their tightly-squeezed ranks of chairs, they listening with the deference due to so great a personage but also absorbed with the thankful recollection that their part in the show was over.

Miss Steele was not there. She was ill, and had been prescribed a long rest. A shadow fell over T-squared's face when she announced this.

The term was coming to an end. Before Christmas there was another event which remains vividly in the memory. It was an era of pageants, and the City parishes had decided to combine and give a succession of scenes from the English past as a charity effort for orphan children. Each church chose its scene, and my father had a clear idea of what would suit his poor and simple parish. It must be something with a large cast but no star roles, with little or no dialogue, easy to act and to understand. Eagerly he seized on the idea of an old English country fair. This might have seemed to a casual observer to be a far cry from a town parish of the twenties, but my father knew his people. His parish was like a village. It was a tight, close community packed into the narrow space in the curve of the city wall. So it was surprisingly easy for the people to translate themselves into the villagers of the eighteenth century that they were supposed to represent. The fair gave them scope, and it gave their parson plenty of opportunity for jokes and merriment. Everything was there — Maypole, pipe and tabor, Jack-in-the-green, pedlar and showman with dancing bear, and the actors threw themselves into their parts with delight. In fact the enjoyment of the fair was quite real and needed very little acting to get the mood across the footlights.

Taking care, of course, not to single their children out, my parents gave me the part of one of the village girls in the crowd. How I enjoyed it! The theatre was already to me an enchanted land, so it was a wonderful thing to find myself on the professional side of those footlights in the Theatre Royal where Shakespearian actors had held me breathless (the names of Forbes-Robertson and Doran having now been added to the list). Excitement mounted as one waited in the wings for the preceding scene to play itself out, then to step on to the stage in front of that dim sea of faces. The after the initial flutter there was that remarkable return of confidence, the joy of giving people what they were waiting for, the pleasure of being part of an action which was itself part of something bigger. No wonder I was a little stage-struck for the one and only time in my life. The world seemed to be beckoning to me from all directions.

And then there was the beckoning mirage of travel. I had never been further from home than Morecambe, and time was already growing short. Soon I would not be young!

> *I wish we could go to Italy! I don't want to go when I'm a fat old lady with half-a-dozen pugs, but now, when I am young, and when my mind and my destiny are forming themselves, while I am yet at school in the Fourth, and still interested — but I shall always be that, I think — in languages, and still alive to the mystery and beauty and romance of Venice and all Italy.* Oh, can't *we,* can't *we?*

III

In January I was fifteen. The groping after self-knowledge which had been so adventurous became now more painful and complicated. It would have been no use to explain to me — if anyone had tried — that the urges and frustrations which I kept so dark were only the common human lot in adolescence. Dissatisfaction with myself darkened the landscape, and what sense of humour I had seemed to fail. Even Winifred, that most comical of wits, seemed more sombre. I noted a sense of maturity about her and a growing cynicism. I grumbled that she was pessimistic, and she turned on me with the words, 'I don't see how one can be happy in a world where one is bound to see one's parents die.'

I looked at her, horrified by this glimpse of truth. My own vision of the future had got no further than the nightly prayer that I and my family might all perish together, go down in the same ship or something and so escape separation. This was of course not an impossible turn of events, but I was far from knowing how indeed likely it might be.

The change which really darkened the February days was the death of Miss Steele. It shook the school. She died on February 6th, *peacefully, just after sleep,* said the diary, voicing my wonder and awe. Death was an enthralling speculation, part of the marvel of life. It had never come near me except when my father's mother died. I had seen her lying in her coffin while my father stroked her unruffled brow as he so often touched the foreheads of the sick people he went to see. That was not a frightening memory but a picture of continued love.

The day we heard the news about Miss Steele was calm and still — like a saint's day. I felt at once we ought to keep it as such. But the event was less important for me in itself than in the state of meditation it produced in my mind, egocentric as ever. I am sorry to say that the surviving memoranda of it are of a rather literary character. The fact was that I hardly knew Miss Steele, who had been a distant figure to me, though obviously venerable. The others, like Winifred, Olive and Beatrice, had known her for six or even eight years; she was part of their youth, the most revered personality of their world.

I had had a glimpse of this one day when Miss Steele had told a girl to come and see her after the lesson for some misdemeanour. Beatrice told me she had looked at her still, ascetic face and 'I wondered if she were praying.' It would have been easy to assume that she was continually in communication with spiritual powers. That such a person should die filled me with desire to know, *to learn for myself the knowledge of immortality that lives among men,* to have some clue to the huge puzzle of existence. But, that I did not mourn like the others filled me with a sense of guilt. Once again I failed to be one with them in their sorrow.

The day of the funeral was Ash Wednesday. After my Greek lesson, I filed out with the rest of the school into the Minster for a Lenten service, then came back to school to the usual time-table of English, geography and algebra. However, after lunch I went with Winifred to the nearby parish church where the vicar was our school chaplain. It was a staggeringly ugly Victorian building. There in the aisle, purple-draped and massed with flowers, stood the coffin with two tall candles at its head. I knelt in a pew between Olive and Beatrice. Soon my eyes began to stray. Winifred's bowed head was immediately in front of me between two other older girls; in front of them were Miss Steele's friends and her three sisters. I could see that Winifred was crying, and so was the girl next to her, Cherry. They were not rivals now, I reflected, but more like sisters. Beside me tears were flowing too, and I felt ashamed. Why did I not want to cry? Why did I feel no emotion at all? Had I really loved Miss Steele? Not to have done so would seem an immense crime; but there was no answer and my mind was a blank, though the coffin was there before my eyes.

Then the Vicar rose to his feet and said: 'Let us thank God for the gift of Helen Steele; for her gentleness, her untiring service, her unswerving friendship, and her devotion to all things good and beautiful.'

And suddenly my tears flowed and I cried heartily for all the rest of the service, scarcely able to sing *The Saints of God* or *Jesus lives* or to see the church which seemed so dreadfully empty when the coffin was carried away.

And then there was another dilemma. Walking back to school with the others after this storm of tears I was still solemn, but there were two possible points of view even about that:

> *I hope I wasn't gloomy afterwards just for show —I know I wanted people to see I felt it. But I was so relieved to find that I could cry, and I did care, that I cried all I could, almost.*

The curse and duty of introspection! Either one was hard-hearted or one was showing off — and whatever the truth might be one was sure to be wrong.

IV

Spring came, with a peculiar charm that year. Again certain pictures stand out. A clear evening, with a star appearing and a pink-primrose flush on the western horizon. The way home from church lay through a small gap in the wall, called a Bar like its large cousins; it had a central arch and two small side tunnels, and the outward face was decorated with a coat-of-arms. This gate had been walled up after a rising and had remained closed from 1489 to 1827. No wonder it spoke oddly to me as I passed through it Sunday by Sunday, though I knew nothing of its history.

One evening in April our party walked home from church up the narrow street, past the churchyard which held Dick Turpin's grave, through the little Bar and past the cattle market towards the wider road dignified by the presence of the War Office. John and Winifred walked ahead, and I made a lagging third, while our mothers and Winifred's aunts came along in a group behind.

'Well, if I did tease you, it was only what you deserved,' flashed Winifred. 'You're a tease yourself, John. Don't forget Aunt Lucy!'

I sniggered. I myself should never forget that ride home from a Christmas party in a dark cab. Winifred was to come home with me, and I had entered into a plot which involved explaining to her that my Aunt Lucy was coming in the cab to fetch us. In the corner of the ancient black upholstery crouched a bundled figure, apparently a very old woman wrapped in heavy shawls. As the cab bowled along, the recurrent lamplight threw a fitful gleam on this piece of human wreckage. Winifred sat in petrified alarm. At last we stopped at the Rectory door. Suddenly Aunt Lucy threw off the shawls and cried 'Now, Winifred!' in as commanding a voice as John could manage. I could never quite remember whether Winifred had screamed.

John tried to look abashed at the reminder, but only succeeded in looking gratified. The other group came up and Winifred's mother asked, 'Well, John, are you going back to Oxford soon?'

'On Saturday,' he said with a little bow. 'It's goodbye for now, I'm afraid.'

'Next time I see you I suppose you'll be wearing your cap and gown,' mocked Winifred as she gave him a cool white hand.

I looked at them both and wondered — at him, so fair-haired and debonair, at Winifred shaking her dark curls with a hint of gold in them, the light of mischief in her grey eyes. It was not the first time I had speculated on the state of John's heart. But this, so common and natural a thought to the teenager of a later generation, was daring to me. Somewhere, just round the corner perhaps, there were other relationships, an adult world — but for me it was far away.

My own relations with people seemed to be worsening. Winifred was still perfect, and always kind, but something was different. The diaries were still full of her virtues and charms, but they permitted themselves a faint touch of humour now and then:

> *Winifred must be a saint. Also I presume she's a martyr!...I wonder if it is possible that I should ever, in days to come, begin to regard Winifred as a friend, and not as an adorable mystery as far away as the moon?*

Always there stood by my shoulder another I, sternly critical and impossible to appease, coldly pointing out my deficiencies and how unworthy of other people's regard I really was. It never occurred to me to rebel, or even to recognise that this voice with the impossibly high standards was also myself. It seemed to be the Sorcerer, bending its implacable brows on the cringing Sorcerer's apprentice.

A widening of the horizon was badly needed. The diary reflected my weariness with the perpetual struggle to please others and myself. Somewhere there must be a loophole into a world where one's efforts would be repaid. Where could that world be?

It became a queer sombre spring. One heard discussed threats of a general strike, and watched men drilling in fields by the river: men in plain clothes with rifles, a sight one had seen before in what we called the Great War. *It's terrible to think they may be used in civil war yet!* the diary said. There was a coal strike, anyway, and five miles away at Stillingfleet stacks were ablaze in the farmyards, and people had a new word for the danger — *Sinn Fein*. The glow from the Yorkshire farms was a reflection from the chaos of Ireland — so much, anyway, I understood.

But at the end of April there was a break in the clouds; my parents and I went to visit John in his first summer term at Oxford.

I had very little idea of what I should find there; no day-dreams preceded the trip. I knew that my father had wanted to take an Oxford degree, but it was flying too high for a penniless student in those days, and he had been thankful to go to Durham instead, so John's entry to Oxford was a vicarious pleasure to him. Perhaps I asked myself what Oxford would be like, but I had not much idea of the function of a university, and I had never in my conscious life been so far south.

Dominus illuminatio mea. The impact of Oxford on my fifteen-year-old mind was amazing, total and immediate. I saw nothing of the modern expansion of North Oxford, the 'base and brickish skirt' did not exist for me. What I saw, in wonderment and reverence, was a city half mediaeval and half Renaissance, full of spring blossom, embowered in the new green of the trees, neither town nor country but both magically fused together to make a natural reality, the thing which ought to exist — the Platonic idea of human habitation. (Perhaps one should always go to an old town in spring; the same magic fusion coloured my first glimpse of Rome.)

Oxford was a place where the past was young, where Learning lived in beautiful buildings, yet had a fresh country air, and was approached, like philosophy for Montaigne, by *'routes douces fleurantes'*. If I had known the story of the Renaissance scholar who met a boar while walking in the woods and dealt with him by thrusting a book into his open jaws and crying 'Graecum est!' I should have thought it typified my feeling for Oxford. The book was a talisman. The confidence it inspired was illimitable — and Oxford, encircled by spring, was the shrine of books.

We stayed modestly in rooms, in a house off the Iffley Road. We went to see John's college, where I respectfully marvelled at his ground-floor study and tiny bedroom. The Warden invited us to tea, in a donnish drawing-room where I felt painfully shy. In the distance we glimpsed a burly figure, with a drooping moustache, disappearing through an archway. John said, 'That's my tutor!' It was impressive, and hard to grasp as something which was actually happening to John, but behind it all there was a powerful pull, the attraction of a kind of conglomerate personality which laid a strong hand on my unsuspecting soul.

The strongest area of the spell was the Bodleian. When we went through the quadrangle and looked at the humble little doorways leading to the Liberal Arts and at the great arches leading to the great vocations of Law, Medicine and Divinity, perhaps I was too ignorant to know what all this meant. But it was with a sense of awe and mystery that I followed on up the shallow oak steps of the staircase, so old and humble, to one of the greatest libraries of Europe, and then through a door into a room lined with bookcases, which was to me only a frame for a showcase containing relics of Shelley — that was a marvellous experience.

I lingered a long time over that showcase because I had a passionate, almost proprietary interest in the *Ode to the West Wind*. The lock of hair, the book found in his pocket when retrieved from the sea, had an aura for me, and we had just come from seeing the memorial in University College, where the sleeping nudity of the statue had embarrassed me a little (yes, one was embarrassed then at fifteen by the human body) but the wrought-iron apple-tree above it had seemed as enchanting as Yggdrasil.

I turned round at last — and there was the real glory of the place, Duke Humphrey's Library. I stood transfixed before the perfect room, staring at it all: the reading-desks in their old cubicles; the painted rafters of the beautiful roof with their receding coats-of-arms. And the smell — the smell! It was the odour of learning, composed of old leather, old parchment, old paper, old dust — and yet not stuffy, but ascetic. Would I ever be admitted to read at one of those tables? What sort of book had one to ask for to get oneself let in there?

There is an excellent memoir of schooldays by an outstanding writer who thanks his stars he was not a male bluestocking. I suppose I was definitely a bluestocking, both by nature and environment. It may be worthwhile to record how brilliant and unforgettable the bluestocking experience is. The sense of the past had always been strong in me, and it was now approaching a maturer stage. Dimly I understood now that the love of the past meant respect for human endeavour, the recognition of a continuing and evolving collective personality. But it would have been logical for this interest to have extended itself to recent times, or to have found equal zest in more distant civilisations, the Egyptian or the Assyrian. What was peculiar was that the dazzling shaft of light which illuminated the past for me fell on the fifteenth century. The mediaeval world attracted me, but rather as if it were my own recent past, a natural background for the edifice of learning which resembled the castles standing so white against the blue sky of the *Très Riches Heures*. I thought about *Learning*, in fact, exactly as the early Renaissance writers did in their lyrical defence of *Good Letters*. It was all a wonder and a wild desire, and no one need be surprised if I took myself very seriously.

The Sunday we spent in Oxford was the first of May. I knew what to do, so I got up earlier than the others and crept out of the house in Divinity Road. It was not far from there to Magdalen Bridge. I found that a great many other people were going that way too. In fact there was quite a crowd, and when I came in sight of the bridge it was thick with people. I pushed my way towards the middle, near enough to Magdalen Tower to be able to look up without craning too much. There were people up there, looking through the traceried parapet, appearing very small and far away. The hum of the crowd quietened down and in the silence you could hear the birds singing. Then the sweet melancholy chime came out of the tower. This was followed by the faint strains, distant and pure and rarefied as if it were coming through glass, of the Easter hymn. A passion of listening possessed the crowd. There was perfect stillness, spread out below to catch the notes dropping from such a height on to the earth. In spite of the strain to listen, it was too soon over. And immediately there was a great shout of birdsong all about, as if the birds had been listening too.

The crowd moved and laughed, and normal life began again. Four young men arm-in-arm, with green leafy branches round their heads, came pushing through like a battering ram of banter. They seemed to me to embody the May morning. It never occurred to me that they also represented something else. We were in 1921; they were the reprieved generation.

In the afternoon John punted us along the Cherwell, past the meadows starred with ladysmocks where the moon-daisies would soon be out, by banks fringed with dipping branches, in and out of the chequered shade. That May was a fine one; the afternoon was warm, lazy and quiet, except now and then when other punts passed us, low in the water, full of girls in summer frocks and boys in flannels, sometimes with a tiny-sounding gramophone emitting unfamiliar voices. Someone said, 'Mistinguett'. The raucous voice, as it died away, seemed to intensify the calm of the drifting afternoon. Later on we heard that an undergraduate had been drowned that day in the river. I never learnt the details, but I never forgot that there had been a black lining to that perfect idle hour.

Evensong in John's college was well attended and hearty, with the preponderance of young male voices. More appealing to the imagination was the weekday evensong in Magdalen Chapel by candle-light. The flickering flames lit up the choirboys' faces as they sang the 104th Psalm:

> *Thou deckest thyself with light as it were with a garment; and spreadest out the heavens like a curtain.*
>
> *The high hills are a refuge for the wild goats, and so are the stony rocks for the conies. The lions roaring after their prey do seek their meat from God.*
>
> *O Lord, how manifold are they works; in wisdom hast thou made them all; the earth is full of thy riches.*

It seemed exactly to express my mood.

On Monday we went to Iffley to see the Norman porch of the little church, so like the porch of the church at home, (though not, as I proudly thought, as fine or beautiful). As we passed along the street near the village school, a sight met us which I had never in my northern city life seen before, and yet it was as familiar as if I had seen it in a dream. Out of the school door came the May Day procession of young children. At its head walked the May Queen in bridal white, the May King all in white too, leading her by the hand; then the Jack-in-the-green, the maids of honour and the train of attendants. The schoolmistress was standing on the doorstep to see them off. They were going to church for a service followed by a feast and a holiday, which had to be on May 2nd because the first that year was a Sunday.

Our time in Oxford drew to a close. I was no doubt quite inarticulate about the effect it had had on me. The only way I could 'confess' my yearnings was by staring in a very obvious manner at a girl riding away on her bicycle with her scholar's gown floating behind her. My mother, observing me, said, half-joking, half sympathetic, 'I think *you* would like to have a gown like that!'

Indeed, the scholar's gown was a powerful symbol. No one told me, and if they had it would have only intensified my desire, that the gown represented a privilege which had only been for one year in the possession of women. Even a girl, apparently, could now share in the inheritance. It was clearly the thing most worth having in the whole wide world.

When we broke our journey at Sheffield on our way home and visited the street where I was born, I looked at the black city with an idea that we had gone on to Hell from Heaven.

THE PAGE'S SOLILOQUY

Now in the heday of my life,
Now in the rapture of my spring,
The world doth burst upon me, rife
With all its gorgeous following.
My mistress hath a queenly air;
Proud heart bear I, when through the hall
Her hand on ivory, pale and fair,
Rests on my arm before them all.
O fair white hand where rubies flash!
Yet for your grace I would not give
One beat of pulses young and rash—
Dreading to love a queen, and live...
Dame Poesy I serve—but she
Far, far above me, deigns no glance;
To touch her rube is not for me,
Her silken glories in the dance.
O two fair queens, by worlds apart!
O two fair worlds, each naught to each!
One hath my eyes, and one my heart—
And both, alas! I may not reach.

Margaret Mann (aged 16)
(Prize-Winner)

IN JUNE

I never saw a bluer sky,
Between the gnarled laburnum-trees,
Or prettier puffs of cloud, so high,
Like swelling sails on fairy seas.

I never saw our poplar trees
More daintily to dip and rise,
Or felt the wonder of all these
With greater force flood heart and eyes.

I never loved sweet England more
Than on this breathless day, which Time
From England's vagrant summer tore,
And set to blossom in my rhyme.

M. Mann

Poems by Margaret Mann (Phillips) taken from the school magazine, the *Chronicle*, 1923.

Chapter Five
Hauntings

I

Back from Oxford I came with one fixed idea. It was clear that it would mean an unremitting effort. Boys quite normally went to university (in those days a considerable sacrifice for less well-off, even if professional, parents) but there was no such sense of fitness about it for girls. I am sure my parents did not underline this difference, but I did. Oxford, if I wanted it, must be reached under my own steam.

It was all the more galling when on the day after half-term I sat down at the breakfast table and caught my sleeve in the handle of the hot-water jug. A cascade of near-boiling water emptied itself on to my knees. A huge scald on the thigh was the result. The agony of it was painful enough, but the announcement of the doctor that treatment would mean lying still in bed for at least a month spelt real tragedy. As my mother was seeing him out, I shed bitter tears of disappointment. I made an effort to keep my acute frustration a secret and smile at the anxious mother who installed me in the little front bedroom I had inherited from John, with its tall window looking on to the busy road. There I lay watching the passers-by, numb with pain and chagrin, reflecting that there was no hope of doing well this term in school. There would be no climbing to the top of the lists in English or French; and as for the subject we had just begun, trigonometry, I would be left far behind. The pain of the scald ebbed away, but the feeling of helpless isolation remained acute.

(How good I was at ill-timed accidents! There was that other time when my bicycle skidded on wet tram-lines and I arrived home with a split and gory chin, to find that the Bishop and his wife were about to arrive for dinner...)

But there were compensations for the scald. The news got round. Next day Winifred came in, bringing books from school, and sat down by my bedside and kept me in roars of laughter. Another ring at the door-bell: it was Olive, putting her ascetic face — the face of a humorous Red Indian chief — round the bedroom door; then emerging entire to tell stories about what had been going on that day in the Upper Fourth.

'Trig?' she said, taking up my worry. 'Well, write a note to Miss Hamilton and ask her for a book, and I'll take it tomorrow.'

Write to Miss Hamilton — the new maths mistress who queened it in youthful dignity and whose quiet reserve made it impossible to think of whispering in her presence? She was very young — probably this was her first post — so she must have had marked qualities of command, for the whole school admired her. Her good looks were so composed that they reminded you of marble, and she seemed deadly serious, but that was probably because it was so hard to keep one's countenance sometimes among schoolgirls. Everything about her was oddly perfect, completely under control, with a distant grace. I wrote the note, wondering what would come of it, and settled back into my only comfortable position with more cheerfulness. *After all*, I said to my diary, *I don't think I mind heaps*. If Winifred and Olive were going to come and see me, and a messenger system was to keep me in touch with what the others were doing, perhaps this accident wouldn't matter much after all.

It was a first indication of what so often happens in life; checkmate becoming the beginning of another game. The road which seems to lead up to a blank wall turns out to have, as my mother used to say, a concealed turning. June that year was warm and lovely. I would crane my neck to look at the street and count the pairs of white gloves, which meant according to my reckoning that their wearers had been to the races. Winifred and Olive came almost every day. It was a measure of Olive's friendship, for she lived on the other side of the town. She brought books from T-squared, who was interested in keeping me busy, and if Olive had had any small-mindedness she need not have helped a possible rival so much. But such a thought never entered either of our heads. Olive was strong and generous and ours was a real friendship which had developed through many days of waiting for each other out of school, and finding it hard to part because there was so much to talk about ('I'll set you as far as the market-place...' — 'And I'll set you back again!').

It was Miss Hamilton's demure, remote personality which was the star in our sky that summer. She was gracious about the accident and sent a trig book and four pages of worked-out examples. We marvelled at her condescension. Mathematically impervious, I wrote a letter asking for help, rewriting it six times until finally it was a laconic note. Next day Miss Hamilton appeared in person, walking down the garden path unannounced because my parents were out and I was convalescent enough to be sitting on a bench under the pear-tree with Winifred, who had just dropped in, and another friend who had been to tea. What was to be done? Miss Hamilton came up, fresh, trim and pretty, and sat down prepared to teach. Embarrassment seized me. Somehow the party must be dispersed. On the pretext of finding the trig book I had been lent, I lured my friend Alice into the house and left her there doing her hair. Then in the nick of time my parents arrived, Mother to take charge of Alice, Daddy to talk to Winifred, and I was left alone to my trig lesson and my bliss.

I listened with half an ear. Miss Hamilton explained things, her head bent over the book. There were delphiniums and orange lilies in the border behind her. My eyes strayed to her wrist, where she wore a gold bracelet, a snake with green eyes and a tiny curl in its tail. How cool, smiling and remote she was, an Artemis figure in my private anthology. She was modern too, in fact she was the first person I had ever seen wearing light coloured stockings, a daring innovation which made the conservative Olive snort with disapproval. But it was part of her poised and decorative personality which stayed in my mind as an admired memory long after the *sines* and *cosines* were a comfortable blur.

'Well, that *is* a sweet girl!' said Mother as the maths mistress tripped way. I could have hugged my mother for so much fellow feeling. None of this made me shine in trigonometry; but oddly enough — or was it really odd? — the scald accident made no real difference to my work, and I did better in those summer exams than ever before.

II

So on one side of the picture things seemed to be going well. Dependable friendship and a shining goal — what more could one want? But there is another side to life, although I was not aware that I needed it. In the depleted world of my teens the male element was largely lacking.

As in the last third (to come) of the century the teenager would seem to be burdened with sex, subject to every kind of suggestion, given to every kind of plain speaking, it is doubly strange to look back to an ordinary schoolgirl's existence in the twenties. For example, no glossy magazines came my way with their persuasive stories of romance. My mother bought a little weekly called *Home Chat* for the sake of its dressmaking patterns. And after reading *that* I felt somehow soiled — not because it was not the most moral of publications, but because it expressed the narrow suburban life of women which was what I feared the most. One was surrounded by a kind of conspiracy of silence; there was no loophole for passion. In those days a popular brand of tobacco used to put a bearded, bronzed sailor on all the hoardings; later in the century, it replaced him by a loving young couple silhouetted against a twilit lake. I rarely went to the cinema, and the rising cult of film stars was alien to my home circle. The very fashions of the day, as one looks at them in old newspapers, have no air of youth to modern eyes. The accent was on ladylike lines, lace, bangles and long strings of beads. The affected pose of a *femme fatale* playing with a long cigarette holder and looking out coyly from a cloudy mist of hair was the world of Colette. Between it and the world of my childhood there was a great gulf fixed; and it would take a very determined onslaught later in life to bridge it.

There was no one in the least likely to offer that. At this point I knew no boys at all; my brother's friends had drifted away and my school friends seemed to have no brothers, and, if I ever sat on the garden wall on a summer evening and tried to imagine a lover coming through the branches to meet me, he wore the costume of an earlier age. He existed only in books.

It was all the more strange as it had not always been so. There was the younger schoolfriend of John's with whom I had played a great deal before the age of twelve. I thought his pale features and curly dark hair rather appealing, and was gratified to be allowed to look at his aeroplanes and sail toy boats with him in the bathroom. Long before that there had been the memorable party given by a maiden lady living near us who had a white-bearded father and a plenitude of this world's goods but not the thing she coveted most; so she gave children's parties, splendid ones with all the concomitants, cream cakes and jellies and games ending with *Sir Roger de Coverley*. There were few parties in our lives and this was a special treat, though one tended to be sick beforehand with excitement if not sick afterwards with jelly (the kind hostess was not to be blamed for this). At one of these parties I was struck by the splendid presence of a certain boy. I was about six, he a little older. Whether it was the blue blazer with brass buttons which caught my eye, or the real distinction of the young face, or some quality of leadership which made him stand out for me, I never knew. But there it was — no one else counted for me — except my brother, of course. When we got home John told our mother ruefully, 'I'm afraid she doesn't understand Postman's Knock — she wouldn't let anyone kiss her but me and so-and-so.' I never forgot his name, though I soon stopped asking my parents where he lived. Alas! I never saw him again — but stop, I did see him many years after, looking out of the Lord Mayor's car, and I thought I had not been mistaken.

In the important years, what relations I had with the opposite sex inspired me with fear rather than anything else (fathers and brothers ruled out, of course). An example of this occurred that very summer.

We had been lent a house in a neighbouring country town for an inexpensive holiday. It turned out to be a pleasant place, if a little claustrophobic. But the owners of the house had thoughtfully spoken about us to their friends. As a result John and I were invited to spend a day with these new acquaintances. John was twenty, and seeing no reason to accept an invitation which held no charms for him, said he was not going. But someone *had* to go, if only to keep my mother in countenance, and inevitably it was I who would be the agreeing sacrifice to the proprieties. It was with misgiving that I agreed. I was to spend more than one day with the Browns. It was sheer torture.

Now it must be said at once that this was not the fault of my well-meaning hostess. She had a family of boys and merely looked round for companionship for them. She must have thought that if she threw open her house to solitary young newcomers she was killing several birds with one stone. She could not know what I myself did not know — that the time was unpropitious on both sides.

In those unoccupied days of that hot summer, in that strange shut-in little town, I was being eaten up by a secret clammy misery, recognisable only years afterwards as physical desire. I had no idea why this was so. On the worst days I thought of myself as wicked, on the best as inadequate. I was in a state of suspension, waiting for life to go on, dawdling the time away with my reading... making up verses... petting the house's big sheepdog, Tycho Brahe (who got on so well with the cat).

When I went to the Browns' house I found it cheerful and not alarming. The picnic she took us on might have made a happy day. But Mrs Brown had taken on more than she knew, and the silent heavy-jawed schoolgirl I was must have seemed to her a difficult proposition. Her boys were home for the holidays from their public school. Older than I was, they seemed to me almost young men. They were boisterous, flippant and keen to talk about football — being as much at sea with girls as I with boys. No vestige of a common interest was to be dreamed of. I believe they would have been just as cagey if I had been pretty. More perplexing still, they had a much younger boy staying in the house whom they had brought with them from school, and he seemed to focus all their attention, like a pet. He was a beautiful little boy, and one day they dressed him up as a young Rajah, in a pink turban with a pearl dangling on his forehead, and laughed when he pretended to lord it over his admiring hosts. Without in the least understanding why, I felt a deep sense of loneliness and insult. There was no one to tell me that this was outraged femininity. I remember trying to gatecrash with a joke, by asking him if he knew the national anthem of Siam (*O Wa Ta Na Siam*). This rightly earned me a good snub. I retired in despair.

Why should they bother about a girl, and one with spots and bitten nails and defeatism gnawing at her soul? When another schoolgirl joined the party, also like me at *l'âge ingrat*, it was a great relief. She was not very interesting, but at least willing to talk, and there was a common ground in the lost familiar Elysium of school. Still, in terms of contact with the male, this experience could not have been called a success.

Sexual difficulties were things you didn't discuss. A little later than this, my mother made me a coat of some whitish woolly material, very fleecy and warm, but with the rather baggy pear-shaped line of that year. Unaccountably to her, I wore it very little. My mother would say wistfully, 'It's such a nice coat, I do wish you would wear it,' thinking of the hours spent on sewing and the price of good workmanship. But still I did not wear the coat. What I could not tell her was that one night in the poor streets of the parish, a rude boy had shouted after me, 'Goin' ter'ave a baby — 'oo done it?' My reaction had been silent horrified shame.

About the emotional life of a segregated school I had absolutely no ideas. I could see that where all are of one sex, differentiation occurs and masculine and feminine qualities emerge. Girls can have virtues which are usually called virile, intellectual objectivity for instance, or they can be totally immersed in themselves and in preparation for their 'feminine' future. I infinitely preferred the former sort. It was as minds, as thinking, questioning beings, that they struck me. And yet what did that passionate agony of separation in the holidays mean? Or that despair of self-questioning about what they thought of me?

The truth is that in such an upbringing all the elements of sex remain uncorrelated. A taboo had been established and I was forbidden to put them together. I was naturally aware of occasional physical pleasure, not recognised for what it was, but somehow productive of guilt and shame; it had nothing to do with love. There were idealisations, *crystallisations*, wonderful depths of understanding and friendship — these experiences having nothing to do with sex. There was the hunger for self-giving, and the horror of losing oneself — that push-and-pull which gives some of the frothiest comedies in the world — those of Marivaux, for example — their undertone of tragic truth. And there was of course the ignorance of precise details which came from the discretion of elders and also, quite simply, from never having been in a biology class.

A friend of mine outside the school, to whose house I went from time to time, had an artistic father. He was tied to a humdrum occupation in an uninspiring neighbourhood, but his mind ranged far away from it, into music and painting, into literature as well. He lived in a private dream-world and perhaps he realised that I did too. Suddenly I was aware that he liked talking to me, and I to him — and I froze. What was it that I imagined — that people had babies by way of the ear, like the mother of Gargantua? The poor man must not have been able to imagine how he had offended; was he to know that he had trodden on the toe of Artemis?

York High School pre-1908.

Miss E. E. Ellett, the first headmistress, and the first pupils of York College for Girls 1908.

Chapter Six
Private Worlds

I

The doldrums were soon over. Moving up into the Fifth Form brought me side by side again with Beatrice as well as Olive. This time we were in a square room on the first floor, looking on to the garden from tall sash windows. There was a sense of harmony about this room and I remember it with a sober pleasure.

The class numbered twelve and I thought that the perfect size; few teachers would disagree with me. It was the School Certificate form and that brought a new sense of urgency. This made me happy because it suited the urgency I felt within myself. Blessed, blessed work! My group was nearing the top of the school, beginning to feel important, with a sense of ownership of themselves and the world about them, and lessons meant something vital now; no more marking time. I kept to my rule never to say no to a poem, but otherwise work took precedence over everything.

In the two subjects which concerned me most nearly, English and French, there were two new mistresses this term. They were a markedly contrasting pair.

Miss Pike was the new English mistress. Unlike most of the teachers who used the school as a jumping-off ground, she was no longer young. Short and determined, she had the idea that to teach girls one must lay down the law rather than attempt to allow them a point of view. One fascinating thing about her was her fringe, which bounced sparsely on her forehead and made the girls ask each other if it were false. No doubt it wasn't, only a remnant of a past fashion. Miss Pike's memory now excites pity rather than criticism, but her brisk methods certainly did not arouse any such soft emotion then. She would bustle into the room bristling with defences, expecting opposition and taking it all in the day's work. Her ideas on the study of literature were ascetic. When there was a choice of literary period to be prepared for the examination, it was Miss Pike and not the girls who made it. They would unanimously have plunged for the Romantics, but Miss Pike said no: they would no doubt read Keats and Shelley for themselves, but what they would never read unless compelled was work from the century of Dryden, Pope and Swift. So the class of adolescents buckled down gloomily to the study of the Age of Reason.

I have an idea — and probably had an inkling then — that this choice of Miss Pike's was not founded entirely on her desire for our good. It might have been due also to sheer unwillingness to read Romantic poetry with fifteen-year-olds. Miss Pike had travelled a long way since she was our age, and it would be hard to say whether she did not know, or knew all too well, what our reactions would be.

As things turned out it was probably the only possible course; it was quite amusing to read *Absalom and Achitophel* and the *Battle of the Books*, when it might have been torture to have to dissect Keats for Miss Pike. But this was an escape I did not appreciate at the time. Miss Pike had other idiosyncrasies, such as a furious distaste for cardinal numbers in dates — one must write October 23rd, not 23, which was 'illiterate' — and she held strict views on the grammatical function of words.

' "Either",' said Miss Pike, 'means one or other, but not both.'

I quoted softly,
*'On either side the river lie
Long fields of barley and of rye...'*

'That will do!' said Miss Pike.

Probably I was one of those who made life hard for her. One day she decided on a showdown. When she met me on the landing outside the classroom door she suddenly stood still and gobbled with rage like a little turkey-cock: 'It seems to me you're spoiling for a fight. Are you?'

The attack was so sudden that I was nonplussed and could only mutter, 'No...'

'Because if you are, I'm quite ready for one. I just thought I'd let you know!'

Head high, she sailed into the classroom, as though she felt she had scotched at least one danger that morning.

Yet there was more true feeling for poetry in her than I credited her with at first. When we came to deal with the *Methuen Book of Modern Verse* — a set book for which I was grateful ever after — she showed unexpected likings.

> *Chimborazo, Cotopaxi,
> They have stolen my heart away!*

Miss Pike liked that.

> *My father died, my brother too,
> They passed like fleeting dreams,
> I stood where Popocatapetl
> In the sunlight gleams.*

'Don't you think that does happen sometimes?' she asked, possibly thinking back to who knows what epoch in her own life, when the mind's landscape had held the only reality. The girls looked at her in horrified

surprise. Or she would draw their attention to a poem of John Freeman's which began:
> *Than these November skies*
> *Is no sky lovelier.*

Again, her pupils did not understand. But Miss Pike, at her time of life, knew what that poem meant.

The new French mistress, on the other hand, was very young, ardent and both humorous and romantic. She had a thin eager face under a cloud of hair and her nose turned up delicately at the end. But her mouth was her most unusual feature — the thin lips conveyed sweetness as well as decision. She was full of activity and sometimes bubbled with fun. Keenly interested in us all, she put up no barriers, her standards were high, and I got few good marks from her; nothing but absolute perfection would do.

There was an Honours system in the school by which three consecutive pieces of work marked *Excellent* (flawless) entitled you to take the exercise book to the Office, knock, and say to the august presence within, 'I've come to sign the Honours book, Miss Ellett.' Then Authority would take out a ledger and allow you to inscribe your name, adding her initials to the exercise book. These entries totalled up to the credit of the House — of which there were three — at the end of term. T-squared made use of these occasions. Once she looked piercingly at me through her pince-nez and said, 'You know, don't you, that to whom much is given, from him shall much be required?' I hardly liked to take these words seriously. However, there was not much signing of the Honours book in connection with my French proses. Not that Miss Marchant was not a good teacher: she was able, and her energy was inspiring. But lessons were ceasing to be merely lessons now; they were the first stages of a long climb towards something called scholarship.

It was in that spring term, in that form-room, that something queer happened to me.

In the lower forms it was the custom to have a book set for holiday reading, on which an essay was to be written on the first day of term. Sometimes these were very light reading, and always fiction. In the summer holidays of 1921 I had been led in this way to read at least one book with care. It was *The Cloister and the Hearth*. There was a good reason why I should read it with particular pleasure. It was an excursion into a world which had been my own for a long time, ever since the influence of my surroundings had projected me into the history of the House of York. (Was it significant that visits to my grandmother often took me to Lancaster?) A story I had written just before going to school focused my attention on the years 1485-7. As a result certain parts of the city were indelibly associated with events which only I knew about, especially the parts I knew best, Walmgate, Fossgate and the market square. The central character of my tale was not historical (I knew enough about historical novels to avoid that) and the romantic halo did not cling about Richard III or the Princes in the Tower; the only authentic characters were Henry VII and the Earl of Warwick, whom my mythical hero tried to rescue from imprisonment. The very few books I had read served me well and the time came alive. Indeed so much so that the fifteenth century seemed as immediate as the twentieth — if not more so — and the great tower of the Minster (finished in 1472) spoke to me with the voice of a familiar friend. It was not surprising at all that my holiday reading seemed to come naturally.

It certainly painted a convincing picture. The hero, Gerard, had not much character but perhaps that was because in contrast his environment was depicted with such brilliant clarity. It seemed amazing that Charles Reade could describe in such detail a world I recognised as true. Where had he got his information from? There was an easy answer to this question. But I did not know it.

When I sat down in front of the essay paper on the first day of the autumn term one question stood out. I set about answering it at once: *What idea of the Church in the fifteenth century do you find in this book?* Obviously there was a lot to say about the luxury of the Papal court and the profligacy of the cardinals and all the abuses which had roused the reformers, but there was also a quiet picture of pastoral care (which reminded me of my home): Margaret and Gerard, after all their adventure was over, living a life of self-sacrifice but united in their care for the poor of his parish of Gouda. The contrast between this working team and degenerate Rome caught my imagination.

The Cloister and the Hearth remains one of the world's great books, in spite of all the mannerisms which date it, the pastiche of mediaeval speech, the easy prolixity, the unashamed sentimentality. Historical novels are written differently now. But it had a touch of fire, it was written with love, and built up of enduring material. The source of all this detail was not mentioned till the very last page, and then obliquely, in the record of the inscription over the door of the birthplace of Gerard's son:

> *Hic est parva domus natus qua magnus Erasmus.*

'History,' said Charles Reade, 'has written half a dozen lives of him. But there is something left for her yet to do. She has no more comprehended magnum Erasmum, than any other pigmy comprehends a giant, or partisan a judge.'

A resounding paragraph followed, in all the splendour of Victorian rhetoric.

> *First scholar and divine of his epoch, he was also the heaven-born dramatist of his century. Some of the best scenes in this new book are from his mediaeval pen, and illuminate the pages where they come;*

> *for the words of a genius so high as his are not born to die: their immediate work upon mankind fulfilled, they may seem to be torpid; but, at each fresh shower of intelligence Time pours upon their students, they prove their immortal race; they revive, they spring from the dust of great libraries; they bud, they flower, they fruit, they seed, from generation to generation, and from age to age.*

Heady stuff for a child brought up on Arthur Mee.

Indeed, this page exactly expressed the vein of my early reading — the idealism of the *Children's Encyclopaedia* which had such a great influence on a whole generation. Greatness was the quality of heroes, who rose in every generation to serve and inspire the world. It went without saying that it was the plain, if secret, aim and duty of everyone to achieve what greatness lay in the realm of possibility. To put greatness and scholarship together — that was the spark to fire the tinder. Scholarship was a hazy notion, but it meant the Bodleian Library, searching and finding, abolishing time, possessing the past. All this was apparently vested in the name *Erasmus*.

I had never met this name before, and the book told me nothing about him, apart from the foregoing rhapsody. It was a name which had an inexplicable attraction. Why it should possess this magnetism for me was not at all clear. Looking back, one might guess that the fictional dream about the fifteenth century had been the prelude to a real affinity. Stranger things have happened. At all events, the name Erasmus had something to do with *me*; meeting it was like coming home.

One day I sat at my desk in a maths lesson, under the eye of the admirable Miss Hamilton who sat at the teacher's desk on the dais, with quiet lines of slogging pupils ranged in front of her. They were working out a problem. My desk was in the second row from the door, in the middle of the room. As I sat there my mind wandered from the equation, and I saw the door open. No one else saw it — I did not expect them to. The glossy cream walls of the classroom stayed where they were, and no head was raised. Two people came in. The first was clear, the second a shadowy companion. The distinct one was dressed in what I took to be the ordinary costume of the reign of Henry VIII. He was not ecclesiastical, which suggests that the earlier dream was still operative. Fair hair escaped from a small cap with a touch of embroidery on it, and in the still youthful face the eyes were kind. I had no doubt about who it was: Erasmus. He came up and stood behind me, looking over my shoulder, scanned the work lying before me, nodded approvingly, spoke to his companion and went away.

I accepted that this event was no vision. When Shaw's Saint Joan stood before her judges and they said to her, 'You know your voices are the result of your imagination?' her reply was, 'Of course — that is the way God speaks to us.' My experience was not to be magnified into a divine call, but it was the result of strong imagination. I took it as that, and was not unduly excited about it, but it was strikingly clear; and it had happened.

The room was quiet. Up there on the platform Miss Hamilton looked out of the window at the slightly moving trees. It was odd that this should happen in a maths lesson — but then one had to get through School Certificate in maths before one could try to embark on a life of scholarship.

At this time I was trying to keep a diary in Latin, and in this I described the costume carefully; it was certainly not inspired by any portrait I had seen of Erasmus: I had seen none. And yet for me it could not be anybody else. I tried to recreate the impression I had of his attitude. I used up my small Latin vocabulary in an attempt to describe what I saw: *facies generosissima, benigna lenisque,* the face of a man 'polished by learning'. Also I tried to convey the quality of the great interest and kindness shown to me. Then there was the remark I did not hear. Nevertheless, I knew its general trend: he had come to see how I was getting on and he was satisfied: one day I should be ready. The dog-Latin account ended firmly: *Bene haec tota vidi, felix!*

When I next had to choose a book for a prize I chose Froude's *Life and Letters of Erasmus*. That showed me I had not been wrong. But that was after both mathematics and Miss Hamilton had disappeared out of my life. That morning in the Fifth Form I knew nothing about my visitor, yet when the opportunity came to read his letters I already was familiar with the tone of his voice.

II

The most important thing in life seemed then to be poetry. (In the sense in which I meant it, it does so still.) I was not abreast of new movements and had only come across one poem of T. S. Eliot — I didn't like it. Still strong in me was the impact of Tennyson, Longfellow and Matthew Arnold. The latest poetry I knew was Rupert Brooke's and that of the war poets, also that of the 'Neo-Georgians'. The only living poet who affected me closely was Walter de la Mare.

I was one of those who *lisped in numbers*. This had begun when I was eight years old and gone on steadily, and the year after my fifteenth birthday was full of it. I copied the verses down in a long ledger my father had given me (new except that some used pages had been cut out here and there). In the end, it contained what I valued myself in the way of my verse-experience, over a period of seven years, eleven to eighteen, the fifteen-year-old entries bulking the largest. The verses were not sentimental: that at least could be said of them; nor were they pretentious in an intellectual sense. They did not usually relate to definite events in my life, though the Shelley relics in the Bodleian figured in a couple of stanzas in May. Very occasionally they reverted to the patriotism of the earliest jottings during the War, or were about historical characters like Napoleon, or a precise place like Venice. Almost always they were the product of a kind of concrete imaginativeness, descriptions of gardens or landscapes never seen, detailed journeys through woods, over hills and beside streams, usually alone, observing with obsessive clearness the flowers and branches which made a fresco or mosaic of the world. How much did they owe to the percolation through my childhood of *Art Nouveau?* Strongly present was the sense of the drama of weather, the changeableness of the face of the earth, sunshine, dusk and moonlight, stars and wind.

There were landscapes empty of figures, hills whose sweeping lines framed a corner of the sea, silent gardens with pools and statues, mountains full of troll-hammering, cliffs raucous with seagulls and yet with no sound of the sea in the eddying tide pouring into their caves. The man-made scenes were more hackneyed: Egyptian temples sinister in the moonlight, Eastern courtyards heavy with yellow roses. Echoes of classical legend and mediaeval story-telling were there. I loved set forms, and practised rondeaux and villanelles, and particularly the sonnet. Adolescent verse is naturally imitative, but I had a horror of pastiche, and never knowingly imitated anyone or anything — the echoes were unconscious. Luckily the character of the sonnet is such that one's models are always noble.

There was little or no outlet for this activity. My mother was always invited to read my verses, and occasionally something made its way to the light through the poetry prize or the school magazine. But the dominant note was secrecy. This is a normal trait of adolescence, but it sometimes also has an exhibitionist side. Not in my case. The poems were not even autobiographical; they did not attempt to express a personal problem, unless occasionally in dramatic form. They were wanderings in a spiritual landscape which was no doubt full of unrecognised symbols, and the words which were always recurring were expressive of a need to take cover: *hidden, secret, stealth, sunless, silent, still*. 'Dim' was a word which had not yet begun its downward trend, at least in my vocabulary, and remained poetic and mysterious, and so did 'strange'. Dawn and dusk, as I found afterwards in the Medici Chapel, attracted me more than day.

Even though the Victorians were so magisterial, I knew there was something limiting in their influence. I was beginning to feel that the language of poetry had reached a saturation point, that it would need rejuvenation from some source or other. But from where?

This misty mirror-image of the world, which gave me every now and then the experience of breathing that upper air called poetry, and the small intimate shock of the awaited word slipping into its place, was the continuous mental background of my life. It combined rather oddly with some of my studies and I am not sure how far it matched with the shade of Erasmus. A separate study could be made of that subject.

III

Outside, there was a world which was not dim at all, full of my father's practical jokes and busy with much coming and going in the Rectory. A whole world of reality lay there, and I was to some extent involved in my parents' lives. The poverty of the parish they worked in was very real in those days, and not properly understood by an adolescent with a head so much in the clouds as mine. The living conditions in many of the houses were very bad, and I heard my parents talking about them, and saw and smelt them myself on occasion. But... Chimborazo, Cotopaxi! It was not for me to seek to change them. Even my parents could not do that. And those conditions had no effect whatever on the esteem in which the individuals suffering from them were held; that I can truly say. Courage, kindness, humour, cleanliness shone like jewels in this dark setting. Sometimes with a spark of sympathetic understanding I wondered about people's lives — how the delicate-featured girl of about my own age, who was the daughter of an off-licence keeper, faced up to the kind of rough house there must have been on Saturday nights, how the bedridden woman in the sunless court managed to pass the days... But I could not really understand.

My own contacts with the parish people were happy ones. One miracle was Patty. She appeared one Sunday morning after church with a parcel which she thrust into my hand. She was a plump, rosy, laughing girl who lived in a larger house than most in the parish, just inside the little Bar in the wall which we passed through every day.

Surprised, I opened the parcel and unfolded the tissue paper and found inside a work of art: a jumper, knitted in the fashion of those days in what was then called artificial silk, in shaded pastel colours which made it look like mother-of-pearl.

'I made it for you,' said Patty, only waiting to see my face and then going away quickly.

I wore the jumper and others followed. Patty was a year or so younger than I was, but she was a quick and expert knitter. I could sooner have flown than achieved such a thing myself.

'Do you think it's all right?' I asked my mother. 'It must take her all her time. Do you think I ought to let her go on?'

'Bless the girl,' said my mother, 'I don't see how you can stop her. She would be very hurt.'

'Isn't it too expensive?'

'Her sisters are all working. I think it's all right,' said my mother. 'I expect they give her pocket money and she likes to spend it in her own way. If she didn't she'd soon stop. What a girl it is! She used to be so naughty in church, many's the time I've pumped her back on the pew and wondered if I'd jarred her spine! And look what she's like now!'

My mother was so gentle that this description of her methods with the Sunday School was ludicrously comic.

Patty's laughing, challenging, mutinous look is easy to remember. She was more like a country girl than a town one, and her bright blue eyes danced. Her relationship to me is hard to analyse. There was devotion in it but a certain protectiveness too, a sense of superiority because she knew more about the world than I did. But I had a different world too and Patty knew that. She was content with her own, but I made a window for her on to another life. Although I gave her presents in my turn, I always had the feeling that she was the giver and I was at the receiving end. Her friendship never wavered. It went on through absence, through her marriage and motherhood, through widowhood and sickness, to her dying day, a steady beacon at the edge of my life. Patty never forgot. She had perhaps amalgamated into her feeling for me all her love for my parents and her gratitude for what they had done, the exhalation of joy which came from them; but in the end it was all for me, and no gift was ever purer or less deserved.

There were jobs I was given to do, and one of these was to take a class in Sunday School. I began with tiny boys, surely the hardest assignment I could have been given, and very badly I did it. The working of their minds was totally incomprehensible to me, and when it became clear that the only way they could bear half-an-hour with me was to spend it jumping out of the row of desks and in again, I despaired. It was better when I changed to older children, girls of nine or ten, whose interest could be roused in something I understood.

On Sunday afternoons I would walk down to the parish, through the small Bar in the wall and along a narrow street past the Roman Catholic church and school, across the old main road where the eastern Bar stood on the right with its strange old timber facings, through the churchyard with its leaning stones, under the arching tunnel of lime-trees past the modest brick tower added in the seventeenth century, past the magnificent Norman porch with its six orders, and finally out by the back gate into Navigation Road. The Walmgate area had been fashionable in the seventeenth century, and there had been long gardens running from the large houses to the mound of the city wall. In the nineteenth century all this had been built up, and Navigation Road had come into being, running down to the little River Foss, past the glass-blowers' factory. A criss-cross of little streets and courts had filled up the spaces. Tightly packed, without water or sanitation except for the common pump or privy, without a blade of grass or a tree, these courts were a triumph of early commercial enterprise. Possibly they were at their worst when I knew them, more crowded than they had ever been, and they were soon to be swept away. Their names varied from the frank confession of Speculation Street to the euphemism of Rosemary Place.

The school stood at the end of a short street, a little wider and less dingy than the others, certainly much better than the courts. There was a playground beside it, asphalted, and the school buildings stood right under the mediaeval wall; the grassy mound from which it rose looked in at all the windows on that side. It, at least, was green. There, rain or shine, the Sunday School superintendent was to be found — the devoted woman had never failed to be there for a long tale of years. She lived at the other end of the town, and toiled on her bicycle twice as far as the Rectory people to reach her objective. After she had opened the proceedings, the young teachers went into small rooms, or corners of big ones, with their classes, and I would find myself in a classroom fitting my little girls into heavy, worn desks, ticking off their names in a register and then getting down to the business of the day. The lesson followed the Church's year, and the children read verses from the Bible, stumbling here and there, sometimes lasping into embarrassed silence.

'Go on, Maggie. What's the matter?'

Silence. And I would hurriedly examine the passage, to see what could be holding things up. Perhaps it would be a word which was respectable in King James's time, and had become indecent to the child of twentieth-century poverty: such a word was 'closet'. Or perhaps it was a phrase clothed in poetry, but to them merely improper: *the babe leapt in my womb for joy*. And so they would go on again, trying to give and understand the message, though I am afraid the teacher had very little idea of how to convey the little she knew.

They were delightful to be with, straightforward and serious, with an uncomplaining acceptance of life as it was. I would try to give it some colour by taking them pictures. I cut up some of the gaily-illustrated books I had had as a child, and distributed blazing scenes of Esther before Ahasuerus, or Daniel in the lions' den. (The book these pictures came from held a far-off memory of the day when I had burst into the room where my parents were sitting, with an amazed cry of discovery: 'I can read without talking!') The relaxing moment of the afternoon came when the lesson was over and I could bring out a story-book, one of those improving tales children collected on their shelves in those days. Some of them were too goody-goody for me, though I was usually willing to be improved, but I took the little girls the more sensible ones. They listened eagerly. No radio or television was there to compete, and *I* was Jack-a-Nory.

One little girl stands out in my memory. Her earnest look fixed itself on me at these times. She was an *Alice* of the poor, with a square serious face, and brown hair falling loosely from the hairband on to her shoulders. I knew she was one of a family of eleven children who lived with their parents in two rooms, or maybe one. But the miracle was that Dolly always had a clean pinafore on Sundays, and clean hands and face. Her mother accomplished the miracle, but Dolly herself was a competent and practical child.

One day the book I selected and carried down to Sunday School to read to them was rather a favourite of my own childhood. It was a sort of realistic fairy-tale about an exchange of personalities brought about by some wave of a wand, which resulted in the spoilt little rich girl and the good little poor girl waking up one morning to find themselves with their situations reversed. In these circumstances of course they acted according to character, and the story rolled along.

The rich girl was called Alethea, and I got rather tired of this high-faluting name. I said to the children, 'Let's call her something else.' But Dolly, who was listening intently, said, 'Oh no, Miss, do go on calling her that!' I looked curiously at the eager little face and went on reading.

The half-hour was over, and I closed the book. 'We'll finish it next Sunday.' But Dolly was almost in tears.

'Do go on, Miss,' she begged. 'Do finish it today.'

There was an urgency in her voice which I never forgot. Did I finish the story and keep the superintendent waiting, or did I say no and leave Dolly hungry for another week? Memory does not say. But I thought about it, and it was a revelation. To me the story had been a fantasy, an amusement, even if it had slightly the character of a parable. I had chosen it without a glimmer of understanding of what it might mean to underprivileged children. To Dolly it was her own dream; to wake up one day in a beautiful bed in a beautiful house, and find one had a rich child's comforts and a rich child's elegant name. It must have been a passionate dream of escape, and no doubt she thought it over for days and weeks. Did it perhaps dance with rainbow wings over the squalor of her surroundings, making a private world for her as delicious and isolating as mine?

Mediaeval timbers in the former Talbot (or Fox) Inn, now part of York College for Girls.

Chapter Seven
Elders

I

'Tell me what *you* did when you left school,' I said to my father.

Sitting in his big Windsor elbow-chair in the kitchen, he was rolling a cigarette, with his deft hands. For this he used a 'machine' — a tube split in halves which he filled and then, after wrapping the paper round it, withdrew one half — and hey presto! his smoke was ready. He lit the cigarette and looked at the end of it to see how it was behaving. I sat on the old settle opposite him, elbows on the table, chin on hands, watching the smoke-rings rise and disintegrate in the air.

He smiled reminiscently.

'Well, I left school at thirteen, you know. I didn't have the advantages you have. I had to go to work.'

'What sort of work?' What an odyssey it was! First the butcher's shop where, in company with another spark of the same age, he was sometimes left by the butcher to sell meat, without a price list — and the boys spent some of the money on ice-cream. But it was not for that he got sacked. One day when the butcher had gone out and trade was slack they spent the time playing Indians with a hanging side of beef. They stabbed at it with the carving knives, but when it fell down they had a terrible job to hang it again and clean off the sawdust. And then, seeing from an upper window of the shop the next-door man sluicing down his yard, they were inspired to turn the butcher's hosepipe on him. That was an end of butchering.

'So what did you do next?'

Next on the list was the chemist's. That was hard work; the half-grown lad had to run the errands and push a handcart with heavy crates on it up the hilly streets of Bradford.

'I used to recite the *Te Deum* in Latin to see how far it would take me,' he said, 'and I kept on forgetting bits so it took me to the top.'

'Latin? You were learning Latin then?'

He explained that he was going to night school at the Church Institute. The teacher, who had been an army officer, could roll off whole chunks of Ovid; this seemed a tremendous accomplishment. Homework posed a problem; the family home was a small house in a terrace and there was no room to be alone, away from his three sisters and brother, all younger. Fortunately the house was in the middle of the row, next to the wide covered passage which led through to the rear. In that passage he would walk up and down reciting *Amo, amas, amat...*! And so he learnt his Latin verbs.

'Did you know then you wanted to go into the Church?'

'Yes, of course — that was why I was learning Latin.'

'What gave you the idea?'

'Mother Church,' said my father with serious sweetness. 'Mother Church taught me. I used to go to church, with my mother, and that was how I knew.'

He told me that as a little boy he had always felt his mother to be different from all the other boys' mothers. She was somehow more *beautiful*. And remembering Granny, who had died when I was twelve, I understood what he meant. She had a rare refinement of feature, a quiet dignity, a faculty of laughter which had no sharpness in it. She was in a way like a queen, yet she spoke Yorkshire and was a working man's wife. It was she who gave me my Shakespeare.

Her son's departure from the chemist's shop was her doing. She had found a medicine bottle in his pocket, filled with the drippings from the barrel in the cellar; what the beverage was I'm not sure. But Granny's principles on inebriation were firm. Grandad had once ordered a barrel of beer on his own account, but when it was brought to the door she stood on the clean whitestoned step and commanded the drayman to take it away again. 'I'm not having that in my house,' said Granny.

The chemist called on her after the bottle episode and offered to take her son as an apprentice without premium; but Granny said no.

What did he do then? Growing up a little, he got a job on the railway. Railways were booming. The house where he was born, which had belonged to his grandfather, was demolished on the construction of the new station. He became a porter, which meant getting up at 4.30 a.m. to start work at 5.0 a.m., to finish at 5.0 p.m. An accident cut short this part of his career: one dawn he was knocked down by a train backing into a siding with no lights. With a damaged foot he was in bed for weeks. The family received no compensation. Neither he nor his family knew he had a right to it. Perhaps, in their independence, they would not have claimed it anyway. But he had no desire to return to that job.

The next step was a shoe shop. He was soon sacked from there, for showing impatience with a customer — he was not cut out for trying on people's shoes. He said that after a busy Saturday night the manager had offered to overlook the misdemeanour — but he had no desire to go back there either.

The wool trade was the obvious attraction in Bradford. For a year he worked at wool-sorting, for a boy's wage of eight shillings a week. All the time he was working hard at his books, staying up late, going early to work.

From this firm he left of his own accord. He took a pride in doing the work well, and one day he had built up a wall of fleeces in the approved manner, when a disagreeable foreman came along and found fault, pulling out a fleece here and there. In disgust the lad said, 'Do it yourself then — I've done!' and walked out.

In another wool mill, however, he was able to earn a man's wage — up to thirty shillings a week in good times. He went on with his studies. Now it was Greek, with the grammar propped up against a wool bale while he had his lunch. The other hands passing by would enquire, 'What's that?'

Finally, he joined the pressing-and-cleaning business where his father was manager. He worked till midnight and got up at four or five o'clock to study, sometimes working all night long. He was saving up. During this period he even tried a tutor but found him less than helpful. As he ploughed on, the savings grew — in spite of the fact that he gave a tenth of all he earned to the Church.

He was a sociable young man and liked dancing, glee-singing and long walks in his few holidays. On one of these he met the girl under the gig umbrella. Then he discovered that her home was in Morecambe where his own grandmother lived, also his young step-uncles who were fishermen in the Bay. One of them, like him, had ambitions for the Methodist ministry, but he was drowned while my father was still a boy. The memory of Uncle Joe was with him all his life.

So the pattern formed, but in front of him the goal grew clearer and clearer: the University, to take a degree in theology.

It seemed to me a wonderful story. Listening closely, I watched the fine features and bright blue eyes he had inherited from that mother, and the beautiful hands which had done and still did do so much manual work, which could also write Greek, pen good English in near copperplate — and could baptise and consecrate and bless.

II

Looking back, the summer of 1922 seems like a central point, the anchored moment of my schooldays. For one thing it was the year of my first serious set of examinations. The thought of that shut out self-questioning; all one had to do was to get on with the job. Peace descended hand in hand with hard work. Never had living seemed so natural, personal relations so simple, surroundings so harmonious. Syringa, delphiniums and orange lilies bloomed in the garden where I sat, and the tall poplars whispered over my head. The old city outside gave a sense of permanence.

In Minster Yard there was a house where lived two remarkable old ladies. Perhaps they were not so old by modern standards, but anyway clearly venerable. The elder had been a headmistress; she was tall, sweet-faced and stately. The younger was small and birdlike. They belonged to a family well known and long established in the city. Their brother was Master of a Cambridge college. Long afterwards, I met him too, when he was really old, and he told me, 'The disease of our family is longevity.'

During a short absence of my parents I went to stay in Minster Court and savoured the atmosphere which clung to that house. Partly, it was the air of inherited culture which came from beautiful worn possessions and quiet nineteenth-century authority. Partly, it was something much older. The house was Elizabethan, though the great central hall had been divided into smaller rooms and other alterations no doubt had been made. I appreciated being invited to do my homework in a small ground-floor room looking out on to the Court and the Dean's garden. I well remember the elaborate plaster ceiling full of birds alternating with Tudor roses.

The back of the house looked into a narrow garden, opening out as it ran up to the mound of the city wall. We were in fact bang over the angle of the Roman military headquarters. But no centurions disturbed my dreams. I was more interested in the albums of exquisite water-colours which my hostesses' father had left behind as memories of European travels: Swiss villages and Italian hill-towns, delicately sketched in the days of chaise and diligence. However, kind though they were to me I was perhaps a little in awe of Miss Elizabeth and Miss Emily.

Something of the same atmosphere clung to my godmother's house in the country. Here it was rather different in that we were frequent guests and the alliance rested on old friendship. Mr Stock was my father's old vicar, known to him always as 'the Abbot'. Mrs Stock was tall, fresh-complexioned, benign under the roll of white hair brushed smoothly up from her forehead. They were childless, and she mothered the guileless Abbot, whom she called 'Mews'. (Whether she was addressing him as one of the Nine or referring to her love of cats, I never discovered.)

They had gone to this country living after a lifetime in towns and found the East Riding people formidable at first — they were both southerners. The rough frankness of the northern parish puzzled them.

'I think they must all be Danes,' said Mrs Stock.

The parish must have been equally nonplussed by the old-world character assumed by the Vicarage, which now housed Victorian furniture of heavy black wood with carved animal's heads on the arms of chair and settee. There was even a 'sociable' and tables with thick carved legs. As well as mirrors and other drawing-room niceties, there were old water-colours and trinkets from Italy. A thick slice of the nineteenth century was preserved in this house. And the two devoted maids who had come with them were in my eyes completely typical: Sarah, the cook, stocky and red-faced and irascible (though never so with me) and Rhoda, the housemaid, small, white-faced and quick-moving, rather resembling Cocky, the stuffed parakeet, with her sharp nose and fair hair under the starched cap.

The parish had been willing to welcome them in its undemonstrative way. One farmer was heard to say bodingly, 'Well, let's hope this lot'll *sattle.*' On enquiry, it proved that he regarded the last parson as a mere passing visitor, since he had stayed only eleven years.

The Abbot and his wife were goodness itself. I could never imagine a cross word between them, and never, never a disrespectful one from me. It was easy to smile at their unworldliness, and my father occasionally played jokes on the Abbot, telling him incredible things about motor-cycles; or once, when a sheep had strayed into the Vicarage garden, writing him a pompous letter purporting to come from a solicitor about the penalties for sheep-stealing, which had the poor Abbot quite worried.

But it was impossible not to love them, and through them their idealistic, solid-principled age. My favourite picture of the Abbot comes from a day when he had learnt that Queen Mary was to pass through the village on her way to Harewood. He heard the news only an hour before she was due. Immediately he went to the village school and shepherded all the scholars out to stand in a group at the church gate, with himself standing in the middle of them holding an immense bunch of red roses he had gathered from a bush in the churchyard. As it approached, the Queen's car drew up at the sight of the old church, the white-haired Vicar and his little parishioners. Delightedly he presented his bouquet.

It was a different past which fluttered round their house. Mrs Stock in particular was an embodiment of a certain Victorian style, full of kindly solicitude in a world of unchanging principles and social divisions. Her father had been the land-agent of a country family, and her manners preserved a certain elegance and her speech some of the characteristics of that ambiance: like others of her generation she said *larnch* and *gairl.* Her faraway childhood stood on her bookshelves in the volumes of Mrs Ewing.

It was through my mother too that the perfume of the Victorian age was well known to me. She had had a better start than my father as far as education went, boarding-school and art classes, and she had a strong feeling for literature; it was she who read Milton with me in my pre-school days. But the poetry which went deepest and stayed longest with her was that of the Victorians — Tennyson, Browning and their contemporaries. She had two little volumes of Coventry Patmore, and in one way *The Angel in the House* coincided with her vision of the role of women in life. Its mingled tenderness and humour pleased her; I remember her quoting the passage where the young husband on the honeymoon watched his bride collecting pebbles by the sea shore:

> *Her feet, by half-a-mile of sea,*
> *In spotless sand left shapely prints;*
> *With agates, then, she loaded me;*
> *(The lapidary called them flints).*

The glint of amusement in her eye misled me. The quotation was deeply meaningful to her, expressing a childlike wonder, the transformation of simple things into precious ones by the power of love. For Mother, gentle and almost self-effacing, possessed iron self-discipline and brilliant psychological insight, and had schooled a passionate nature. In another volume of Coventry Patmore I found in her handwriting a quotation from Mme de Stael: *Jamais, jamais je ne serai aimée comme j'ai aimé.*

Her girlhood had been passed under the domination of an imperious mother, and this, together with the recognition that she herself also had a possessive streak, had made her put all her passion into leaving others free. She never asked questions, but lent a willing ear. She never gave unasked advice. With her, one was conscious of power, an independent mind and gallant courage, masked by the gentleness of the small figure, the deep brown eyes and demurely parted hair.

This paradox was clear in her relations with her husband. From the moment when he first saw her at the age of twenty, she had been the only woman; his dependence on her was matched by her deference for him. The code in which she had grown up set strict limits to a woman's sphere of action; she was to be the arbiter of household decisions but not to make any incursion into wider fields. She was to be past mistress of household arts, but not to attempt any specialisation. The heaven of devotional life was open to her, the world of menial tasks joyfully accepted was her own; it was rather a monastic ideal. My mother's power came from accepting it out of deliberate choice.

I watched the perfect balance of her life with love and hopeless admiration; such abnegation was not for me. On the other hand her importance in the house was immense; my father never took a decision without her; she was the mainspring of the concern. When he came in he would at once ask 'Where is she?' And no one needed to ask who.

Another country rectory played a part in my life that summer. The Bishop went on holiday and offered us his house in a quiet village, where my mother struggled with an unaccustomed kitchen and I wandered in delight round rooms full of books, trying to read Schiller. On Sunday, kneeling in the old church, I looked through the vestry door into a tiny interior lit by early morning sunshine, where a Jacobean table, a gleam of white linen, a row of shining oil lamps seemed to be still in the far past.

At the bottom of the garden there was an ancient tithe barn, perfect and satisfying with its warm brick wall, its oak rafters and row of hollyhocks, and the paddock next to the house was purely Shakespearian. The way the great trees reared themselves up out of the thick grass, with their roots exposed, gnarled and spreading, their trunks grooved like classical draperies, sturdily planted in the tussocky meadow, gave me an indescribable pleasure. I would sit on the wall watching the slanting evening light thrusting between the trunks and making long warm shadows, down to the little brook:

> *Such sights as youthful poets dream*
> *On summer eves, by haunted stream.*

My verse had changed character. It was not a secret world of half-lights any more, but an attempt to express joy, the brilliance of summer — high white clouds in the skies and tossing white-and-green of poplars, a peace of mind which accompanied me to Olive's home on the Yorkshire moors and back again to the streets of the city in autumn, when the tang of September reminded one that a new school term was beginning. I rode my bicycle through the familiar ways with ecstasy.

Across the bridge, as I looked down to where the dark river washed the white walls of the Guildhall, past and present seemed swirling together in the stream:

> *On thronging streets, with lamps aglow,*
>   *The dusk is falling fast,*
> *Beneath the bridge black waters flow,*
> *By stone facades and doorways low,*
>   *Fruits of a royal past.*
>
> *The lights are rippling on the stream,*
>   *And under a crimson sky*
> *A second bridge's contours seem*
> *To rise beneath the fitful gleam*
>   *Of a moon but born to die.*
>
> *And I, who ride in the falling light*
>   *To a barrel-organ's tune,*
> *Have no less joy in each sound and sight*
> *Than a Greek pacing Athens' terraces white*
>   *Beneath his votive moon.*

Chapter Eight
Influences

I

Dear friend, how much you will have to bear with me now! This is the most difficult time to describe, the solemn priggish years. It would be cowardly simply to laugh at them — indeed I think that would be a great betrayal. They were full of sincerity, if blinkered. One can only try to recapture that curious time.

The last two years at school made a different pattern. It seemed to be a new era, with new anxieties, a climate in which things looked less real the nearer one got to the apparent realities of the outside world. Life felt harsher, yet lit by bursts of triumph or enthusiasm, rather like a walk in an unknown country in changing weather, with distant sounds of church bells or rolling drums marking unexplained events far away.

The Latin diary, still in use and a trifle less doggy *(linguam meam 'caninam' esse metuo!)*, remarked laconically, *In puellis praesum.* In fact it came as a surprise, indeed a doubtful decision even in my eyes, to make me head of the school. Perhaps Authority thought it would do me some good. It was a duty taken with deadly seriousness. Perhaps I was a little astonished myself at the absorbing nature of power. *O potestas potentissima!* Clearly, responsibility was a school in itself. Every day one learnt something new; as the diary remarked, *gratias Deo refero, per diem enim disco.* Luckily there was much kindness about, with my attempts to organise other people being met with tolerance.

Looming up ahead now was the question of the future. The School Certificate was over, and well over, and the small Sixth Form eyed its prospects. In spite of much talk about the emancipation of women there seemed to be nothing open to one, once the hurdles of Higher School Certificate and university were leapt — but teaching. If one were more adventurous, one could be a missionary. But despite early leanings in this latter direction — due to a confusion between missions and exploration — it became clear that I had no vocation there.

We discussed careers. Olive, as usual, had the word of good sense.

'It seems to me that one is either interested in things or in people. I'm interested in people.'

This sounded a rational attitude. But how did one know which one was interested in? And was there not a domain in which things and people were so bound up together as to mean the same thing? I had no views apart from one blinding desire, to go to Oxford. That was looking far enough, and to my eyes it was a huge pinnacle to be scaled. No one from my school had ever gone to Oxford. But it was not that factor, but the financial obstacle which seemed enormous. It was understood that boys must go to college. The diocese might help a parson's *son* — but girls were another matter. I became quite clear in my own mind that it would not be right to ask my father for the money. £250 a year for three years — it was colossal. And the effort of collecting it appeared like taking a header for the moon. The only hope was to win a scholarship.

Oxford was a value that stood by itself; one hardly asked what one would go there *for*. The rest of life lay beyond in a kind of golden fog. But one potential conflict was emerging: where did *poetry* stand? Oxford represented scholarship, which no doubt had its aesthetic side but meant ultimately the use of the intellect for discovery. I was beginning to feel there was a clash here, and that my private slogan — *Oxford and Poetry* — with which I lulled myself to sleep, contained an embedded contradiction. Was there really a great gulf fixed between the analytical and the creative? So far they had seemed the same thing, and to fight for the one was to safeguard the other. But as work went on, became more sophisticated and more absorbing, there seemed to be somewhere in the future a tug-of-war. A little more clearheadedness might have shown me that the tension was a result of my limited definition of poetry. Naturally I did not expect my poetic experience to remain what it had been so far, a kind of private diary crystallizing moments of vision, depression or joy. In any case I already was aware how much sheer hard work was needed to complete the first spontaneous expression of an insight. But still it was essentially a personal voice, very different from the magisterial tones of scholarship. In some way the two had to be fused together, and I could hardly see how. The only thing to do was to go on driving both horses and hope the chariot would get off the ground.

In one of his books, Vladimir Nabokov writes of the surprise felt by the character who sees that the answer to all questions of life and death, 'The absolute solution... was written all over the world he had known', though during his lifetime he had never seen it; his brain being 'encompassed by an iron ring, by the close-fitting dream of one's own personality'. That close-fitting dream is the dominant memory of these two decisive years of mine. Awkwardly shifting ground, yet holding good, remembering that to preserve one's life is to lose it, yet arrogating to oneself the right to lose it as one chose; to forfeit perhaps cosy domesticities and the accepted life of women for a dream, a dream that might well prove to be vain — echoing the poet's ironical words,

> *La belle ambition et le rare destin!*
> *Chanter, toujours chanter pour un echo lointain,*
> *Pour un vain bruit qui passe et tombe!*

In reality the severe discipline of learning with its rewards earned by conscious effort was the necessary ballast for the vague blind striving towards inspiration: without it my boat would have carried too much topsail. But I did not accept this peaceably. There seemed to be another possibility, like the garden behind Wells's green door, a world one could penetrate if one gave it one's all, but which would accept no compromise. The fear was born earlier, but grew in these years, that perhaps I would not go all out for the best, would not be able to burn my boats; and continuous internal self-exhortation kept such fear alive in my mind.

II

The isolation of adolescence (hugged to one's heart as a superior state), although able to take peaceful forms in my life, was nevertheless very much there.

Walking with my family in the Lake District in the spring when I was seventeen, I heard the water-talk of the Greta babbling over its stones at the foot of Skiddaw; what it spoke of was my future. In Crosthwaite church we sat and listened to a preacher fulminating against the times and comparing current politics unfavourably with those blasted by Isaiah; but I was occupied with the fancy that the marble effigy of Southey might sit up and join in.

In a word, it was characteristic of the moment, and of me, that the presence of Southey's transfixed handsomeness on his tomb should enrich the whole picture. But was it right, I wondered, to be made happier in the house of God by a reminder of worldly fame? And what did I know of Southey anyway? Was it mere romanticism which exhilarated me, with no real foundation? Was it *that* which had to be cleared out of my life before I could finally grow up? It would be a wrench comparable to the farewell to pretence games that I remembered forcing on myself at about twelve. Instinct said that the comparison was untrue, that the power of the imagination, which I called poetry, was a lifeline that one must never abandon.

In so far as there could have been a generation gap this would have been the great division. But there was no such gap because my mother too inhabited the poetic world. It was impossible to think that the older generation had stepped over the boundary that divides the unique experience of youth from the shared experience of maturity if one lived, as

I did, with a person who had never parted from unworldly values, only deepened them as she went along.

So it was not a matter of generations — and yet it did seem necessary to find a friend who would share tastes and discoveries and if possible ambitions. Someone else who only wanted to write poetry; there must be someone like that in the world. That spring I thought I had found the person.

Miss Marchant had already been almost two years at the school. She had seen us through our examination, and had begun a Sixth Form course in French literature. We enjoyed Molière and La Fontaine and accepted solemnly her careful notes on the controversy at the heart of *Le Cid*. (She was not far away from her university course and tended to apply its content to her schoolgirls.) The predicament of the Horatii as seen by Corneille was unexpectedly interesting. Miss Marchant was a good teacher and the remote world of the seventeenth century began to move and live. But it was not till I reached the comparative independence of the Sixth Form that I came to observe carefully what sort of person Miss Marchant really was.

Looking back on this experience, I see it depended on two colossal privileges. One of these was the possibility — offered by the *small* school — of purely individual treatment. It is curious how my experience suggests standards and values exactly opposite to our current educational practice. Today huge numbers of pupils and a large Sixth Form are among the criteria of a successful school. But my school was small; its classes, though certainly of 'mixed ability', never contained more than twenty-five pupils. The Lower Sixth during my time consisted of eight (if I'm not mistaken) while the Upper Sixth had an august four. The result was that we could all have the undiluted attention of T-squared and her staff, and very often our lessons amounted to individual tuition — the great privilege of the rich in all ages, but the joke being that we were not strictly speaking rich at all.

The other privilege was linked. Individual tuition had its completed value only when the teacher is able and willing to give with full hands, and to give the riches of personality as well as learning. Miss Marchant was one of those who gave *herself* as well as what she knew. So my real acquaintance with her began in the little room the Sixth Form occupied, a long tunnel-like place ending in one of the Victorian pepper-pot towers, where the window looked out on the best view of the Minster, the south-east corner — one saw the great central tower diagonally, the Early English south transept, and the Perpendicular jutting bay in the choir, a wall of lacelike glass. It seemed the most satisfying view in the world, but on one particular afternoon I doubt if I bothered with it. I was alone with Miss Marchant; the text before us was selections from Pascal.

I could not remember afterwards how we had shifted from Pascal's experience to our own, but after a while Miss Marchant was telling me the history of her religious life. It was a story which began with other people, a little Jewess, a saintly parson...and led to a culminating personal revelation, which was still blazing in her mind. As I listened and watched her glowing mobile face, I was reminded of the description in the *Acts of the Apostles* of the face of Stephen. Since this time I have been confronted time after time with people who have had the sort of experience she was describing, although she, aged twenty-four, was one of the most articulate. At home I lived in an atmosphere where the sense of the presence of God was never far away; it was part of the air one breathed. But Miss Marchant needed to tell of her new knowledge and was anxious to share it; the immediacy of the contact never ceased to astonish her, the discovery of a permanent relationship with Christ was something that gave a new dimension to her world. There are no words to describe this adequately, but she came near enough to communicate something of her joy.

Next day I went out into the garden and found her supervising recreation. It was May. I imagine it was a calm day of early summer, with white clouds drifting high in the blue sky over the Minster roof. In the confined space of the school garden there was a general hubbub. Girls were everywhere, loitering and laughing, hailing their friends, running in and out of the French windows of the room where milk and biscuits were to be had, standing about in talkative groups. I threaded my way to the corner where Miss Marchant's chair was drawn up to a small table with exercise books for marking on it. She looked up at me with her tight-lipped little smile, a trifle lonely in the midst of this unheeding noise.

'What are your books?' she asked.

I put them down on the table: *The Oxford Book of French Verse;* J. W. Mackail on Latin literature.

Miss Marchant fluttered the leaves of the anthology, and suddenly we both exclaimed at the sight of one particular little poem.

'I do love that,' I exclaimed.

'So do I,' agreed Miss Marchant, and she read in a low voice the few lines of *Ronsard à son âme:*

>   *Amelette Ronsardelette,*
>   *Mignonnelette, doucelette,*
>   *Très-chère hôtesse de mon corps...*

I suppose she knew what I did not, that it was a translation of the Emperor Hadrian's address to hs soul. The soft ripeness of it in sixteenth-century French delighted me.

'*Ne trouble mon repos: je dors...*Yes! And what have you found in the other book?'

'He talks about a poem he calls the *pervigilum Veneris* — do you know it?'

Miss Marchant's eyes lit up; of course she knew it.

'It's the most beautiful poem,' she said. '*The Eve of St Venus,* I've heard it called. It has a refrain — *Cras amet qui nunquam amavit*'

I finished it for her:

'Quique amavit cras amet.'

That page of Mackail had made a deep impression on me, linking as it did the almost modern cadences of the late Latin poem to the spring-time sweetness of early English —

> *Betwen Marche and Averil*
> *When spray beginneth to spring...*

But never before had I met anyone who could enter into that delight.

The only person I had been able to talk to about poetry was my mother but she could not follow me into these linguistic explorations. It seemed now as if the friend I longed for, the person who could share the sheer rapture of rhythm and the fascination of language, was there at last. Talking about these things in the crowded playground brought all my lyricism on to the pages of the diary. It was like standing alone with her on a peak, *on a peak of Eternity*, said the diary, *while below us and about us rushed the eddying flow of the world and Time*. Yes, it was as exciting as that. What I had found was not only a kindred spirit but a born teacher who could kindle others and be kindled herself at the sight of their delight. And it came on me like a spiritual passion.

Work had always been alluring, now it was transfigured. Even set books for the examination took on a glow of inspiration. It was so with the *Georgics*, which exhaled a fresh smell of trees, and gave out flashes of colour and sudden pictures: the grey-green leaves of the willow, the white oxen ploughing, the towns perched on the high rocks and the rivers flowing beneath old walls,

> *Fluminaque antiquos subterlabentia muros...*

Verse came to my aid for translations of Horace or Villon or Victor Hugo. I picked up a school copy of the *Chanson de Roland* on the second-hand bookstall and the dying prayer of Roland at Roncesvaux haunted me:

> *Veire paterne, qui onques ne mentis,*
> *Qui Daniel des lions guaresis,*
> *Et Saint Lazare de mort resurrexis,*
> *Guaris de mei l'aneme...*

I wore the back off my little copy of Shakespeare's sonnets. Even having to 'do' it for examination purposes could not spoil *Antony and Cleopatra*. I discovered Browning, Francis Thompson, more Shelley, more Keats. But no doubt Miss Pike was right, and it was better never to have an examiner's claws on the *Ode to the West Wind* or *To a Grecian Urn*.

Life was extremely magnificent, even if sometimes devastatingly uncomfortable. My untrammelled childhood had left me with two characteristics, a conviction that one was only living when one was busy with the creative process; and an inability to regiment my thoughts. Whatever struck my fresh senses produced a vision of glory — and this had to be expressed *somehow*, often lamely enough. There were days when I waited in passive obedience for the right words to be offered by the subconscious to complete the pattern, to fit the translation — and what a pleasure it was when it came! Such exercises, like mental chewing-gum, kept the jaws of the mind busy. But if ever they stopped, in rushed the uncontrollable anxieties, the sins of omission or commission, real or imaginary, the assumption that others were contemptuous or hostile, like a battle horde —

The multitude that would be one life's lords.

My mother could often exorcise them. But adolescence has its own sadness, and it came over one most often in the hours of leisure — sitting perhaps under the trees on the playing-field near the tennis-courts waiting for a turn to play, idly watching the rhythmic passage of the balls across the court, listening to the *ping* of the catgut, a sound which meant summer, but.....

III

As the summer holidays approached, an unprecedented thing happened. I see myself on the afternoon of July 2nd, looking in the letterbox behind the front door in answer to the postman's ring. I took out an envelope for Daddy, an unsealed 'nothing' — but there was another deep in the back of the box. Miss Marchant's handwriting — and addressed to my mother! I remember I had to get tea for my father and a visiting cleric as my mother was out — out for two mortal hours. When at last she came home the contents of the letter were revealed: an invitation to stay at Miss Marchant's home in a nearby country town, for a week of the holidays. Beatrice was invited too. Nothing had been said at school so as to avoid disappointment should it not be possible for us to accept.

Next day I took a letter from my mother to school. I met Miss Marchant on the main staircase, sacred to staff and senior prefects. On the landing she put down her briefcase and read the letter, her thin, humorous, spiritual face framed by the black oak of the old panelling. Folding up the letter she said vehemently, 'Good!'

'It's awfully sweet of you' I began.

'It was really my mother's idea, you know,' she said cheerfully. (This rather damped my spirits, which recovered as she went on.) 'I must have talked about you to her oftener than I knew, for one day I was talking to her about another girl and she said why not ask you? And I said, oh, I'd love to! But we've had it in mind for a long time.'

It was hopeless to explain what joy this was. Delighted conferences with Beatrice followed. But in the next few days those attacking hordes came on, not yet quite understood for what they were: fears, incredulities, self-deprecation. Was it possible to accept such hospitality and not be gauche, clumsy, self-conscious? I wished I had Beatrice's frank ease of manner and gift for saying what she really meant. This was too important an event not to go wrong somehow.

Mother understood. 'Why not ask her to tea?' she suggested. So Miss Marchant came to the Rectory. I was all anxiety as I introduced her, but — as so often — I need not have worried. A specially good tea was an auspicious beginning. My father's blue eyes woke responsive twinkles in Miss Marchant's, and she seemed suddenly to be sitting there like an old friend.

After tea he had to go out but the rest of us stayed chatting on the step outside the French window, which my father had extended so that we could have tea there and watch the sun westering, golden behind the branches of the great elms. It was a curious place: on the left ran the long whitewashed side of the kitchen and outbuildings, on the right a flower border backed by an ivied wall, and in front of us the straight asphalt path leading to the wider part of the garden. Overhead, the tall poplars — one of them gigantic — waved their heads ceaselessly, and the elms spread fanwise against the western sky. It was very secluded and quiet there. Miss Marchant talked. That happened with Mother, who somehow made you feel she sat beside a well of quietness, and because of that could give you her full attention, undiminished by any thought of self.

A scrap of that talk remains to me. Miss Marchant owned to unfulfilled ambition.

'If only one could really do something for the service of Christ.. if one could be of any use...'

Mother looked at her visitor.

'I think the great thing is to be ready,' she said. 'If one is ready, the opportunity will come. One has to keep the lamp trimmed.'

'Oh, do you think so?' Miss Marchant's eyes lit up. She too, as I can see now, was in a formative moment of her youth.

The visit was a success. 'We can't see too much of nice people,' was my father's verdict, like a benediction. The other visit by Beatrice and myself duly took place too. It was queer to see her in her own background, to meet her father and mother, to think of her as a person like other people. I went through these experiences in a somewhat dazed state. Beatrice was more practical and more mature.

One day on a walk in the country, we sat down to rest on a hillside. Below us lay a valley, 'embowered', as I should have said at that time, in trees, and a pretty village nestled (there really was no other word) at the bottom. Miss Marchant looked down at the scene, at the trees heavy with the foliage of summer, the roofs, church-tower and ivied walls.

'That might have been my home,' she said reflectively.

I thought she meant it might have been her parents' home, but Beatrice knew better. She looked up questioningly.

'Yes, a young doctor. But it wouldn't have done.'

Wondering comprehension dawned on my mind. So Miss Marchant had actually thought of getting married. It had not occurred to me that the sacred race of schoolmistresses ever did. Moreover, this particular one had seemed like a disembodied spirit. The world of poetry which I was trying to share with her was one in which marrying and giving in marriage, the ordinary tenor of life, simply did not exist! Somewhere there was a great gulf to be bridged. Suddenly I felt the limitations of my childish world, and left Beatrice to do the talking.

This jolt did not spoil my relations with Miss Marchant. It simply gave her an additional touch of glamour. She moved in regions as yet forbidden to me.

Later in the summer she paid me a return visit. We went for a walk to a neighbouring village, idling along beside the cottage gardens bright with hollyhocks, peering through the railings in front of the Hall. Its Elizabethan facade with double stair pushed out dark wings at the sides, pierced with diamond-paned and mullioned windows, and on the sills the motto ran: *Garde la foy*. In the grass-grown courtyard Goujon's Diana stooped to caress her fawn. But she was no business of ours.

The churchyard, bordered with huge trees, was cool and inviting. We lay on the grass there, looking up at the white spire against the blue sky, and talked of marriage.

'I wouldn't mind getting married,' said I, 'but what a nuisance it must be to have children!'

'But you don't need to have children,' Miss Marchant responded, gazing at the point of the spire.

'Don't you?' I asked, waiting for more.

For a moment it seemed as if Miss Marchant was going to say something else. But she only turned over and began to pluck stems of grass, and chew them meditatively.

IV

The rest of the summer holidays are a kaleidoscope of small experiences, each with a large significance. In adolescence one swings from adult ambition to childhood longings and back again, a very confusing sequence. I missed my friends; leisure was often torture because it opened the gate to the torrent of doubts and worries. Secure at home, I was wildly insecure in my public relations.

Exam results came in, only Subsidiary papers this time, and afforded a momentary satisfaction. One of them had been a French translation paper which made me marvel at its unfairness. Did those examiners know what they were doing? The passage was about a mediaeval walled town. I did not know a number of the technical terms used, but I only had to think myself into the streets of York, imagine myself in front of a Bar or walking along the Wall, to get the whole description right. But what about the candidates who had never seen a portcullis?

One Saturday morning I wandered as usual about the market. The old bookstall beloved by my father was there, and I bought two volumes of *Gil Blas* and a parallel French and Italian grammar, all for threepence. At the pet stall I was completely carried away and spent five precious shillings on a tiny liver-and-white mongrel of spaniel descent, only to find on arriving home that the family was due to leave for Morecambe on Monday. Ignominiously I returned the dog to the stall but did not recover the five shillings.

To Morecambe we went, and there as usual my spirits swung up and down like the tide. Here was the enigmatic house — and Grandma. And the familiar bits of odd-shaped limestone along the front garden wall, the long path at the back leading through the yew arch past the yellow daisies into the quiet little orchard with the sharp apples. Over there were the Lake mountains, blue and flowing — and in front of them Arnside Knott and Wharton Crag, which I tried to draw. There were letters; one was from Olive, particularly heart-warming with its reflection of the steady light of friendship. That at least was surely solid, anyway.

Did I ever (does one ever?) suit my reading to my surroundings and needs? During that holiday I read Racine and also went to the performances on the pier, noting in my diary, *The pier at night.* '*O Susannah!*' *Came out feeling wholesome once more*, or *Went to* Chu Chin Chow. *No one liked it but me.* But the great discovery of that time was Alfred de Vigny. I bought *Journal d'un poète*, and found myself completely fulfilled in it. There was I, in 1923 still a schoolgirl, living in circumstances which were surely favourable: a home where harmony reigned, where parents loved and were beloved, where I was free to spend my time as I wished, enjoying a mental world which seemed full of colour and riches, crowded with the friendly faces and heroic words of the past, and as far as my little attempts had gone, being met with success. Yet the disabused Romantic's was the voice which really came home to me. *Le règle de la vie est le deséspoir.* The valuable things seemed to be reserve, control, resignation, being master of one's fate even by opting out — the only answer to the battering of the inner life, the storms of hope and fear, the longing for adult love and the searing heat of ambition which one concealed fiercely from everyone.

If only I could have known him! mourned the diary. *But anyway I've got the book.*

Chapter Nine
Ending

I

Just before the start of the autumn term, I went to hear a famous poet and writer lecture at a boys' school in the town — Walter de la Mare.

As usual the diary was frank: *It wasn't the lecture I went for, but the man. Such a delightful shock to find how ordinary and human and charming he is.*

But I didn't really find him ordinary at all. Still young, he was pale and slim, with a dark elf-lock on his forehead. He spoke with elegance and simplicity about poetry. I hardly listened to what he said, and did not remember a word afterwards. He was a *poet* — the first poet I had seen in the flesh, and I knew him for a real one. What I listened to as he spoke was the voice of my own heart. Sitting alone at the back of the hall, I regarded the person to whom God had given the gift I prayed for. Oh, I knew well enough that it was a gift of pain, something which meant the sacrifice of everything, so that nothing in life would remain the same — that you had to buy it as the pearl of great price or, as I put it to myself, *you had to burn your boats*. But if you did, you would get your heart's desire. It was an article of faith with me that if one wanted anything enough one got it — provided, of course, that one's faith did not fail.

Fortunately it was not the time yet to enquire whether I had that faith. I merely listened to the poet's voice and stumbled out into the September evening, feeling 'too serious for life', fatally divided between ambition and self-ridicule. One self watched the other with cynical derision, but the positive self was the stronger, and its transport was so strong that mind seemed to rule body. And I trembled (says the diary) *from heart and soul outwards...the great passionate Endeavour shakes my being as if it were the most fragile of things.* The entry ended in an incantation: *O God, make me have it all in me — make me have it, O make me, make me have it!*

There could not have been clearer autosuggestion. And the discomfort which accompanied it was a kind of obbligato to the fierce thrumming of the demand. It was a genuine demand, and it canalised the passion of adolescence. Poetry was the supreme experience, and more than an experience — it was a myth-figure, an angelic power, a daemon, a thing not earned but given, coming to one from outside, and one's whole duty was to receive it with an open ear. It was a flash of clairvoyance, married to the extraordinary assumption that one had the power and the right to make words into something new. Sometimes one had to work at it, but oftener to wait, and some of my verse came near to automatic writing. But it was sporadic, uncontrolled, over-simplified, using old images and childish thoughts and vague urges: *the gleams and glooms that dart Across the schoolboy's brain.*

Then there was the necessary world of work. On October 2nd I went to the postbox at the corner with a letter. It was a lovely autumn day, with a sky that was deep blue overhead and barred with silver-grey fleeces which then turned into clear tones of marble and peach in the west where dark lines crossed the sunset. I dropped the letter into the box. It would make a difference to me; would it be important to anyone else? It was the application for Oxford.

Guaris de mei l'aneme! said the diary. *Now for Cicero.*

Cicero, Virgil and others occupied me as I sat on the old settle in the kitchen, with my books piled on the table in front of me. Head propped on my hands, I followed the defence of Milo, or put into blank verse the beginning of the *Georgics*, all about the different species of oak or the ways of the willow, or the ode of Horace beloved of schools: *Integer vitae scelerisque purus...* The priest from the Community of the Resurrection who was staying in the house for a parish mission would come in and say jokingly, 'I don't think you're really working, you know — you're only pretending.'

Father Hall was as joyous a monk as ever existed, but he was no Friar Tuck. Very tall and thin, he arrived on a bicycle suited to his great length, with his sole luggage, a parcel wrapped in what we called American cloth, wobbling on the carrier. His worldly possessions appeared to consist of two large silk handkerchiefs, one red and one green, which he used alternately, washing one every day and hanging it on the back of a chair to dry. He had no money, apart from a small allowance which he sometimes spent on sweets. His utter freedom made a deep impression on everyone at the Rectory. A lady missioner arrived too; she was a parson's wife, and equally gay.

During the days of the mission the house rocked with laughter and the church filled with people. My father was cautious in his assessment of the permanent effect. He thought, no doubt rightly, that few lives would be radically changed, but even these few were of importance; and he felt that the invisible results might be more important still. He was not a man who relied on violent decisions or sudden conversion. I remember a seaside holiday when we went to morning service (Sunday was a busman's holiday for him) and heard a revivalist sermon of a particularly crude kind; my father took a strong dislike to the preacher and to a teenage helper who was with him. Seeking a better experience, we went to another church for Evensong, but the same preacher and the same acolyte were functioning there too. That evening my father was buttonholed by a middle-aged lady staying in our boarding-house, who had been driven to horrible misgivings by the preacher's assertion that only the moment of blinding conversion can make a Christian. He talked to her on the verandah of the house, far into the summer night. I never knew what he said, except for a few strong words about the wickedness of a view which could push people to despair. But I can imagine the sane and sunny confidence with which he dispelled her worries. To him there would be many ways, some gentle and some cataclysmic, for the hand of God to be laid upon us.

It remained true that the mission was a concentrated form of what was going on round me all the time. Father Hall was seeking to do by shock tactics what my parents were doing by continuous precept and charity: to bring to ordinary struggling people the vision of God.

> *And lo! Christ walking on the water,*
> *Not of Gennesaret, but Thames!*

The people who came to listen — the shopkeepers and factory workers of the parish, the schoolmaster and his wife, the postman with the fancy waistcoat, the two very different chemists, the girls who worked at the chocolate factory and the people who made small livings at the shoe-shop and the draper's, the woman who had a rag-and-bone business and turned out to be one of Father Hall's permanent converts — they knew well that their parson and his wife were the real thing.

Here was an ideal of life very different from the one my passionate longings sketched for me. Here was instant acceptance of the work to be done, self-fulfilment in self-abnegation; joy because a choice had been made and no further uncertainty was necessary or possible; freedom because there was no need to consider self. It was an activity which knew no boundaries between matter and spirit, equally expressed on the one hand in the heartfelt sermons and the administration, unique each time, of the sacraments and, on the other , in the management of the cross-grained church stove with the cinder-raking and wood-sawing of which my father's life was full. In the same way those delicate artistic gifts of my mother's had been applied to the hardest physical work of a large Victorian house, without losing their effect on the world round them. There, under my nose was a way of life, fully integrated and complete. But to them, my absorption in my work and dreams was a vocation too.

At present, I could evade the issue. Conscience was quiet, because it really looked as if hard work — to develop one's mind and learn to seek truth — was the path of duty. About the verse-writing, I might have had more interior discussion. In a way it was a selfish pleasure, and the hope of fame pure egotism. And yet it wore the face of duty too. And to feel that it was not to be had without great sacrifices was theoretically an equalising factor. So

I lived in an atmosphere of encouragement at the Rectory, understanding what my parents did and yet taking it for granted, absolved from much active participation by my successes at school, and by their way of assuming, as I grew up, that my road in life was to be different. Indeed, when once I proposed to open a Sunday School in premises which had fallen vacant in the poorest area of the parish, my father, who knew those streets better than I did, said no.

There was another aspect of the religious life under my eyes, though I hardly thought of it in those terms. T-squared began, for her Sixth Form, a most marvellous course of the Hebrew prophets. Never again could any of the class look at the Old Testament as a flat landscape. It revealed itself as a series of perspectives, each adding a new shaft of light. Isaiah, Jeremiah, Amos, Hosea each contributed his special insight into a many-sided vision, growing before our eyes. It was impossible to think there was any connection with the revelation of Jesus.

There was no trifling with T-squared, who remained astringent even though she was able to convey this brilliant picture. Perhaps most of the girls never emerged from the state of distant respect for her; occasionally a particularly clear-sighted one moved from an early condition of near-hatred to one of admiring love. That is probably the usual history of Mother Abbesses among their flock. I remember on this occasion an embarrassing negative proof of the awkward strength of her personality. Towards the end of the term we had an oral examination by a canon, and everybody was anxious to do her credit; so that, when it was discovered that she was to be present, and she took up her seat by the window, at a distance from the long table where the class sat round, a general feeling of dismay swept over her pupils. It was impossible to act naturally, as if she were not there.

The canon looked round genially, and put his first question. It must be noted here that at the very beginning of her course T-squared had warned us against the vulgar use of the word prophecy. 'A prophet in the Biblical sense does not foretell the future. He is the channel of the word of God.'

So when the canon said, 'Well, and what is a prophet?' it was with dread...a perverse pleasure...as though submitting to a fatal compulsion, that I replied immediately, 'One who foretells the future.'

T-squared dropped her head into her hands. The other girls stared at me: had I gone mad? I was supposed to be the star pupil — how could I say such a stupid thing? The canon smiled. 'No, a prophet is one who says, Thus saith the Lord...'

When T-squared asked me afterwards how it had happened, I answered miserably, 'Because you were there!'

And perhaps she understood.

II

The entrance examination to Oxford came in the late autumn. I sat for it alone. The teachers read my papers with curiosity and trepidation before sending them away. There were French and Latin papers, a wild General Paper which caused me horrified amusement by containing a question on *clocks*, and an Essay paper with a choice of four or five subjects. One of these I seized on with eager delight: it was Shelley's dictum, 'Poets are the unacknowledged legislators of the world'. I think I had no idea at all what it meant, but it was a peg on which to hang all I thought about poets and poetry. 'Your essay was awful,' the teachers told me afterwards.

But somehow the people at Oxford decided to put me on the interview list, and I set off one day in early December, accompanied by mother. The whole thing was a new and exciting jaunt and I would think my mother enjoyed it as much as I did. The South was scarcely more familiar to her than to me. We leant out of the window to buy buns from the boy shouting what sounded to us like 'Barnberry kikes!' with a pleasant feeling of being in a foreign land. When we arrived at Oxford Mother went to an hotel in Beaumont Street — and I went on alone to the College.

The College had a humble entrance in those days, through a double door next to old cottages and what had once been an inn, the Waggon and Horses. Behind these there was a gravelled drive and more cottages, then a rather dignified porch giving on to an entrance hall hung round with noticeboards. Putting down my bag and feeling like an explorer in the jungle I looked at the lists till I found my name. Apparently I was to have a room for the night in Library Passage. Someone kindly pointed out the way, and I unpacked my bag in a little room with a casement window opening on to a large lawn studded with a few big trees. It was peaceful there in the mild December dusk. The room contained a desk, a wicker armchair and an upright one, a cupboard on which stood a jug and basin, and an iron bedstead with the coverlet rolled up to look like a divan.

I had seen from the lists that I was down for two interviews, one after dinner, one next morning. There was plenty of time. A maid brought me hot water in a can, and I changed into the frock a kind friend had warned me to bring. It was a short frock in golden-brown poplin with a lemon yellow lace collar, and I hoped it would do. I was making efforts now to look grown-up, and my rather sparse mouse-brown hair was screwed up into a bun, very difficult to keep pinned up. But, as I was told afterwards, the little brown frock conspired with my snub nose and unsuspecting brown eyes to make me look about twelve. Powder was unknown in my world, so it must have been with a face shining with soap-and-water that I emerged from the room at the sound of a bell and shyly made my way to the Junior Common Room.

A few girls were there already, sitting on the edges of chairs, and the atmosphere was that of a dentist's waiting room. At last I could bear the silence no longer, and said to my neighbour, 'I say, I think we ought to get to know each other's names, don't you? I'm Margaret. Are you having your interview tonight?'

The other girl looked at me coldly. 'As a matter of fact,' she said, 'I'm Up Here.'

'Oh!' I gasped, not having realised that a few first-year students would be in residence for Pass Moderations, 'I'm awfully sorry...'

This was evidently a second *gaffe*.

'I don't know what you're sorry for,' drawled the girl, 'unless you think you'll be Up Here with Me.'

This had its desired effect and struck me dumb, so that it was lucky that a group of dons arrived just then and swept us into dinner.

Very different, fortunately, was my second human contact, the interview with the Tutor in French. After dinner, at the appointed time, I found my way to her first-floor study and knocked on the door. These small things had to be done — but what an effort they cost!

The response was a brisk, cheerful, 'Come in!', rising at the end like a bird call. I found myself in a room which seemed to be lined with books from floor to ceiling. A bright fire was burning in the grate, and behind a desk strewn with papers sat a person with a delightful gnome-like face. Light hair was brushed back from a high forehead and I perceived a large mobile humorous mouth and twinkling, compelling, sympathizing eyes. Taking the chair she offered me I suddenly felt immensely happy. This was obviously the real person I had come to see. This was the Oxford Don.

How very lucky I was I only fully understood a number of years later. But already I knew that my confidence was justified: Oxford must be the place I had imagined, since it produced people like this. I had no difficulty in recognising the Tutor as a person of vast intelligence and learning, with a strong devotion to truth — but she was also human, funny, and able to give me her full attention, thus conveying the impression that there was no one else in the world for her at that moment. The feeling that she was so deeply good produced automatically the best possible version of oneself while in her presence. No wonder she liked people. They were transmuted into gold by her interest, the true philosopher's stone. There was no difficulty in talking to her. In the space of a quarter of an hour she must have had a complete idea of the very green young person who sat before her.

In fact she suggested that it might be better for me to have a year abroad between school and university, and try again for Oxford a year later.

'Has anyone suggested that to you?' she asked. 'Sometimes people get a great deal more out of their university course for having had a year's experience first.'

Resolutely I shook my head. 'I don't want to cost my parents any more. I must pay for myself as soon as I can.'

There was one more thing she had to find out. Pushing a book over to me she asked me to read a page of French. I did so, painstakingly. I had never been to France.

'I see,' said the Tutor.

The interview could have gone on all night as far as I was concerned, but nodding pleasantly at me she brought it to an end. I stood up. Then with a burst of courage born of her kindnes I put the question: 'Do you think I've any chance of a scholarship?'

'I should think your chances are practically nil,' was the reply.

Such was the attractive sincerity of her character that the words did not strike as harsh nor irredeemably disappointing.

'You see, the College is not rich. There are only six scholarships. But we must wait and see.'

Thanking her I left, exhilarated rather than dampened. Back in Library Passage, I undressed and knelt beside the bed to say my prayers. It was just ten o'clock, and all the towers in Oxford seemed to be striking the hour. The air was full of bells and as I listened it was certainly the Oxford of my imagination which lay round me, the magic city where truth matttered and nothing else, the age-old home of beauty and thought. Arnold's famous lines were no platitude to me: 'spreading her gardens to the moonlight, and whispering from her towers the last enchantments of the Middle Age' — for that was exactly what was happening on that first night of my first isolation as a person. As the sound of bells came to me across the College garden I felt a confidence in this

Towery city and branchy between towers.

Next morning I had an interview with the Principal. She was a famous classical scholar and a great lady. She was kind too, and looked at me encouragingly from under the shining roll of grey hair which topped her tall impressive figure. But that interview was shorter and seemed more of a formality. My courage never flagged again. I danced my way back to Beaumont Street and into my mother's hotel with a lightness of step. When I could not keep my blithe spirits out of my voice as I told her, 'She thinks my chances are practically nil...' Mother was frankly puzzled.

Back I went cheerfully to Corneille and Cicero. After all, Higher School Certificate was not very far away, looming like a mountain. I did not worry about the Oxford result; it seemed enough to have had such an experience and seen such people. The verdict came quite soon in a letter signed by the Principal, and it was an offer of an Exhibition of £25 a year. Although a positive result, I found this confusing.

'But that won't get me anywhere!' I said to T-squared. However, she was radiant.

'Of course we must think how you can get some more money — but this is a start, don't you see? You must accept it — unless you want to try for

Cambridge in the spring?'

No, I was adamant that it must be Oxford. So, after accepting the offer with suitable gratitude, I waited to see what further miracles could produce the vast additional sum of £225 a year.

III

During the Christmas holidays I spent a large amount of time typing out my verses on my father's old Remington. I had decided to send some of them to a man who advertised in the newspaper: *MSS for publication required*. He answered my letter politely, and told me that if I would send him forty poems they would be considered. Finding forty was an easy matter, but typing them out with two fingers took days and days.

January came, and the new term. The last term but one, and how the familiar scene was sharpened by the sense of passing time! The smell of the floor polish in the school corridors. The new glass-fronted bookcases on the landing which were to be the nucleus of the Steele Library. The staircase — scene of my one April Fool joke. The re-arrangement of one's possessions in the long narrow Sixth Form with its turret window. The dry humour of Olive, dependable and just; the mixture of idealism and sophistication that was Beatrice. The lovable Yorkshire bluntness of the girls from the country. The increased respect in the eyes of the younger ones. The Olympian feeling which belongs to Sixth Forms everywhere.

One day early in the term, I arrived at school with a headache. I had nearly decided not to go at all. I performed my first duty, that of ringing the bell for assembly in the classrooms. Then I went upstairs and met the others; at seven minutes past nine it was time to ring the bell again, and we all went down to prayers in the Hall. I was surprised to see Miss Marchant sitting at the piano as she had been away with 'flu. How tired she looked!

Thursday was nearly all free periods now, but I needed some books from the classroom where I saw Miss Marchant again. Her thin face lit up as she gave me a gentle 'Bonjour'. Up to the old house's attic with Olive and Beatrice I went and tried with head still aching to do a French unseen. After an English lesson came another free period. While I was waiting for Beatrice in the corridor T-squared came by and asked what I was doing.

'I have a free period, Miss Ellett.'

'Where are you going?'

'Into the attic.'

'You could go into the drawing-room. No one is using it now, I think.'

This was unaccustomed dignity. Beatrice and I went to work among the luxury of polished tables and chintz covers. I took up the notebook in which

I was supposed to be writing out Dr Johnson's views on Shakespeare — a selection of criticism being one of our set books.

But Dr Johnson was fated to be neglected that morning. I found myself telling Beatrice about a wonderful conversation I had had in December with Miss Marchant. We agreed in our estimate of her as one of the most selfless and idealistic people we had ever met.

Tracing round one of the chintz patterns on the arm of her chair with a blunt pencil, Beatrice said, 'I'm afraid she's not very happy just now.'

'No, I thought not,' I answered. 'But I don't know why. Do you?'

Beatrice was silent for a moment. Then she seemed to make up her mind.

'Yes, I do know. I don't think she would mind my telling you, because you like her. She's...well, very much in love with someone. Only—'

'Only what?' I asked, taut with concentration.

'Only he's ill. Too ill for them to marry, perhaps ever. That's why she looks like that.'

I drew a deep breath. 'And yet she's just as kind as she could be!'

Beatrice met my eyes. 'Yes, she thinks of everyone. She never stops to bother about herself. I think she's marvellous.'

I thought back to that conversation in December, of my own stumbling efforts to convey deep feeling without being 'sentimental', and of the strong hand with which she had dealt with the awkward childish questions about friendship returned. I remembered how I had been reassured, told I was a valued friend, left at peace on a high level of contentment, feeling understood. And all the time Miss Marchant had had this tragedy at heart!

It was not at all surprising to me that Beatrice knew all about it and I didn't. It was natural to confide a love-affair to Beatrice, who was so much more mature. (Beatrice knew a lot of things. A little scene in the classroom might have revealed this to me. I had written on the cover of a private notebook a quotation from Sappho:

> — *querentem*
> *puellis de popularibus..*

and Beatrice saw it. Her eyebrows shot up and she gave me a quizzical glance. I pondered over this. Was there some meaning in the words I didn't know? There seemed to be some cloud or other over the name of Sappho — I didn't bother to explore its origin. Perhaps she was disreputable? Anyway, she was a poetess and that was all that mattered. I did not pursue the question any further. But evidently Beatrice did know a lot of things.)

Now feeling for Miss Marchant was deepened by an agony of sympathy. At choir practice, which she usually took, I felt I understood why she looked pale and tired, and surprised us all by sitting down to listen to our singing instead of standing at the music desk as usual. We sang: *Put thy trust in the Lord, and he shall give thee thy heart's desire. Commit thy way unto the Lord, and he shall bring it to pass.*

In French conversation lessons it was all the more admirable that Miss Marchant would be her own brilliant self. She was an adept at the difficult art of making schoolgirls speak in foreign language with *feeling*. On this occasion Olive was given the task of convincing her of Browning's virtues as a poet; while she struggled with this topic someone put forward the name of Barrie. At once Miss Marchant took up the name in the spirit of the exercise and began derisively singing 'Mary Rose! Mary Rose!' in Olive's serious face. As I looked on, admiring her energy and spirit she turned on me — 'Et vous, à quoi allez-vous me convertir?' I shook my head at the challenge, but she insisted that when the railway strike was over I must come and over tea discuss until we found something I liked and she didn't like, 'et alors vous me convertirez!' But I knew that would never happen. Her vivacity made me tongue-tied; it was with people made of sterner stuff like Olive that my words began to flow.

During that spring I followed Marchy's emotional life from a distance, as it were in a glass darkly. Obviously in that adult struggle there were elements hidden from me, things I could not know and that she could not tell me. All the time I was conscious of a battle, a spiritual and physical battle which was calling on all her principles and all her faith. But at the same time as she was fighting her own battle, she was always ready to enter into the affairs of others.

'Find a moment on Monday to tell me what you hear from that man, won't you?' she flung back as she ran for her train. And I blessed her for caring about the fate of the forty poems.

'I did hear from him,' I told Marchy when we met again. 'But it's no good; he'll print them if I can send him forty pounds. Now where on earth could I get forty pounds?'

IV

The problem remained, however, to raise the funds for Oxford. The Principal of the College wrote a letter in her own hand, suggesting ways of obtaining grants. The City of London Companies helped students who, as in my situation, had an award of sorts but very little else. Applications were sent in and forms filled up. One of these old and dignified companies was known to T-squared because she had been a headmistress in one of their schools. On a day in spring I found myself on the train for London, with my father, this time, in the opposite corner. It was fun to be going to London with him, even for the mixed blessing of an interview.

'Did anything like this happen to you when you went to College?' I asked him.

Daddy shook his head, and began to tell me more stories of his own youth. In January 1897 at the age of 29 he had saved £40 and, ready to burn his boats, went up to Durham to sit for an entrance exam. He had in fact tried once before, but had run away out of sheer fright. This time he left a packed trunk with his mother for her to send on in case he got through. He did get through. The trunk came, and he had a first term at the University. But after that his funds were exhausted.

'So what did you do?'

'I went back home,' he said.

Back home to his parents' cottage in the Bradford of the 'nineties. One evening he met a boyhood friend in the street, his old friend Harry who had recently embarked on a career in the wool trade. Together they went to one of the humbler restaurants of the town, where you got hot peas and tripe.

Sitting opposite each other at the bare table under the gas jets, Harry asked, 'And what are you going to do now, Francis?'

'Back to the mill. I'm going to work and save up again till I can go back to College,' said my father.

I can see Harry picking at his peas reflectively.

'I've got an aunt, you know, Francis. She's quite well off...and good to me — she's just lent me something to help me start a business on my own. Now could you go back to Durham if you had a hundred pounds?'

A hundred pounds! In those days, living sparingly, he could. It would see him through his B.A. course and perhaps to an M.A., and into his first curacy. Harry clapped him on the back with bluff encouragement, and the deliberate Yorkshirisms he was to keep up all his life.

'Pay me back when tha likes, lad. I'm reight glad to give thee a shove...'

Harry had made a fortune since then, lost it and made it again, but he remained the same hearty downright character he had been in his youth. He was John's godfather and had a family of children himself. His letters came, written in a bold flowing hand and full of jokes, exclamation marks and Yorkshire stories. And at Christmas came those bales of beautiful dress lengths from the mill.

I looked across at my father, rolling his cigarette with the deft shapely hands which were just as expert at sawing logs or sweeping the chimney. With a history like that, no wonder he was as ready to tackle any job as a backwoods parson.

He conducted me gaily to the interview, which was held at the Company's Hall in the City. We waited in a vast space (or so it seemed to me) where easy chairs and little tables stood about under the coffered ceiling, and where we partook uneasily of tea and cracknel biscuits. When our turn came we were summoned to appear together before the committee. In a small panelled room a large number of gentlemen were seated round a table, and my father and I were offered two chairs facing them. I suppose I answered a few questions, but I remember well the moment when the chairman turned to my father.

'What will you do if your daughter does not gain this scholarship?'

'I shall borrow the money,' replied my father in a loud firm voice.

I looked at him in surprise — this was news to me — and the chairman said hurriedly, 'Tut, tut, my dear sir!' and bowed us out with the utmost ceremony.

The rest of the visit was comic. A hotel for the night was not to be thought of, so we stayed at a bed-and-breakfast place, a tall house in a square. The beds were all right, but the breakfast included a thick slice of very fat bacon which my father could not stomach. But neither, characteristically, could he bear the thought of hurting the landlady's feelings. So the slice was wrapped up in newspaper and taken out with us to be given to the first hungry dog.

Rain streamed down in torrents. But it did not prevent us from paying a sodden visit to the Empire Exhibition at Wembley, to me a confused amalgam of African villages built of red mud and a life-size statue of the Prince of Wales, complete with horse, carved in butter. We also stood under the dome of St Paul's — and went home feeling it had been an adventure.

The scholarship did materialize, and it was for £60. Another company produced a grant of £20. There was the City Scholarship: if I could merit that on Higher School Certificate, it would add another £80. With the exhibition, that would make a total of £185. But I needed £250. There was one other possibilty, said T-squared: the Board of Education Training Grant for teachers.

'But I'm not sure I want to teach,' I demurred.

'Well, what else do you want to do?'

What indeed! Here was a question. There were my manuscripts lying in the bedroom upstairs. I remembered my father's remark in earlier days, as he read my verses (handed to him by mother). 'I don't know what we are going to do with you,' he joked. 'I don't know any shops where they sell poetry!'

That was really the point. If the products of writing were to be a saleable commodity, dare one expect to earn a living by the pen? Would that ruin the very independence one was seeking? Was it true, as people said, that you could 'begin by teaching' and then find your way to being a writer? But was that an honest approach — to sign a form saying you wanted to teach when not in the least sure? Passionately I felt that I wanted to go into this new adventure free, that a subsidy with strings to it was not what I wanted at all.

And yet, was I going to buy my freedom at the cost to my father of £60 a year? Over the three years I would cost him nearly £200 — more than the yearly stipend from his benefice had been when he went to the Rectory. In my eyes it was enormous.

'You don't have to sign anything till you get to Oxford,' said the persuasive voice of Authority. 'Just apply, and you can think it over.'

'What do you think I ought to do?' I asked my father. He shook his head

— his handsome head, already white.

'You must decide that for yourself. Of course it would be nice if you could accept the money, but I don't want to influence you. It's your business now.'

I knew I was not strong enough to say no, at once anyhow; better make the application and trust to being able to reach a true solution later on. So I sent the application with many misgivings, and wrote to the Tutor to ask if an Exhibition entitled me to wear a scholar's gown.

V

The Sixth Form turret window had no window-seat, but it had a radiator, and I was sitting on that, with the *Collected Poems of Keats* in my hand. Outside, beyond the garden walls and the hidden road, the Minster choir spread its fretted crockets against a sky of marbled cloud. The great central tower looked as solid as a hill, faintly purple like a heather moor, and the pigeons wheeled ceaselessly round it, rising and falling.

It was the last day but one of the summer term. Tomorrow all would be bustle and confusion, collecting of belongings and saying of goodbyes, addresses being scribbled down and holiday plans exchanged, with a shudder of apprehension about the exam results in August.

Lord, dismiss us with Thy blessing... yes, indeed!

Beatrice came into the room.

'Hullo, you do seem to like sitting on that radiator.'

'Well, no one can say it gives you appendicitis to sit on it, when it's cold.'

Beatrice came and sat on it too.

'I say, there's something you ought to know. About Marchy. I've been going to tell you for a week, but I couldn't, somehow.'

'What is it?'

'You know that day she was away last week?'

'Yes, it was Wednesday.'

'Well,' said Beatrice, studying the tip of her gym shoe steadily, 'that was the day he died.'

A great pity gripped my heart. I remembered Marchy's face, no less kind and with no less light in the eyes, but a little tighter-lipped, that was all.

'Oh, Beatrice! What can we do for her?'

'No one can do anything,' said Beatrice, 'except the Lord, and he can.'

'What do you think she will do now?'

'I think she might go to that missionary college she was talking about,' said Beatrice practically. 'Do you remember?'

A memory of dusk closing in as we sat round the piano at Marchy's house came to me — and her voice as she sang to us. We had wanted her to sing again, and asked for the same bit of a cantata, *'O divine Redeemer!'* and Marchy had laughed at this and called us funny children. But perhaps it was the conviction in her voice as she sang that made us prefer that to secular music.

Beatrice went away, but I went on sitting there. My eyes followed the wheeling pigeons, up and down over the Minster roof. It was hard to realise that I was leaving school tomorrow. All the hopes and fears, all the jokes and admonitions, all the other lives, T-squared and her staff, especially (I think now) the little sandy-haired Latin mistress who had tried so hard to help — Winifred and Beatrice and Olive and the rest; surely they would never fade into memories, surely they would always be as vivid in my mind as now? Above all, my heart ached for Marchy. My own prospects seemed unbelievably bright, like a range of sun-tipped mountains, but far away, behind it all, moved the shadow of change.

The garden at the Rectory.

Margaret Mann aged 18.

Chapter Ten
Beginning

I

Summer was a time of waiting...with an uneasy feeling that perhaps one ought to be doing work in readiness for the next term — but what? Mention had been made of Pass Moderations, a course in logic, lectures on De Toqueville... Nevertheless, next term was very much an unknown quantity.

That summer an unprecedented thing happened in the shape of a letter to my father from the Archbishop. He said that *Arnold Lunn* had offered the clergy a number of free holidays on the Continent — would my father like one? Neither of my parents had ever been out of England. They discussed the magnificent offer. It seemed best to choose a cheap booking, not only for modesty's sake but because then it would be possible for my mother to go too. So the windfall amounted to a fortnight in Switzerland, at £9 apiece.

They had at this time arrived at a point of lessened tension, with both children almost self-supporting. It seemed extraordinary to think of them actually amusing themselves, free of care for once. They had a day in Paris, took the lake steamer across Lucerne, drove along the Axenstrasse, thought about William Tell. They even went to the summit of the Rigi and joined in a spontaneous snowballing match at the top.

So the Rectory was empty for that fortnight and during this period John had his own friends to visit. I went to stay with Grandma. This was a curious experience, very precarious — anything might happen. Grandma was a venerable figure in Morecambe, where she had been the first headmistress of the Board School opened under the 1870 Act. She had smacked the bottoms of boys who were now influential councillors and in fact almost everyone in the town had come under her ferule. She was therefore delighted to have an almost-undergraduate grand-daughter to show off, and never failed to mention the Exhibition to Oxford, until I protested, 'Really, Grandma, you're treating me like a prize pig!'

So far, so good, and I ought to have been glad to have given satisfaction. But we fell foul of each other constantly. Grandma's dapper little person, sharply feminine but also adamantine, concealed an iron will and a fierce determination to have her own way. I was now old enough to be equally obstinate. I was not the submissive girl my mother had been. It did not daunt me now to be told to go upstairs and get down on my knees and ask forgiveness for speaking to my grandmother 'like that'. It may be that we both enjoyed these rows. Anyhow, I was able to expend faithfully the money Mother had given me for the purpose of taking Grandma out on rail and coach trips — to Liverpool, to Preston and on the Six Lakes Tour.

That house came near to yielding up its secret to me, but never quite. It could have told me a great deal if my ear had been more exactly attuned. Its controlled, deliberate cleanliness, the scent of camphor in the sea-green parlour with the lace curtains and green carpet encircled by a wreath of flowers, the atmosphere of the living-room with its chaise-longue, glass-fronted cupboards and old photographs, all contributed to an impression of something unspoken. There were steps leading down to a cool, clean cellar, where milk stood on a stone table, with a prehistoric air. In the hall stood a large grandfather clock; in the bedrooms there were illuminated texts on the walls, large mahogany beds and carefully arranged dressing-tables. I remember the white sheepskin rug in Grandma's room. In the bathroom there was always a strong smell of Lifebuoy. (The lavatory was outside.) Everywhere in the house the same dominating influence prevailed. But there was one exception.

It was a large attic, painted white, with sloping ceilings and a dormer window from which one could see over the roofs opposite, into the country. This dormer window had wide sills, wide enough for a person to sit hunched up there with a book. There was not much furniture: a single bed, some upright chairs, a small table painted green and decorated with small wreaths of flowers. And there were pictures. On an easel stood an unfinished portrait of an old fisherman. Landscapes stood stacked against the wall, and a portfolio held a pile of water-colour sketches. The room had an atmosphere altogether different from the rest of the house — a mingling of light, air and freedom.

I often went up there with a book. Sitting in the dormer, with my back against the side panes and my eyes on the distant view, I would dream rather than read, or look back into the room and savour its faint strangeness. Why was it like this? Why did Grandma's potent influence cease here? Was it the refuge of a timid but steadfast girl, engaged for years to the young man of 'Goodbye, umbrella', who seemed never to get any nearer to his fixed goal? Was it here that she had gained strength to resist pressure? Was every line in these sketches a frail bulwark against the attacks of the world? My mother spoke rarely of this struggle, but she once told me that she would have given up many a time if it had not been for his buoyant certainty that in the end all would go well. For these were Victorian lovers, convinced of the claims of filial duty. No matter how many insults were heaped on the impoverished suitor, he would not have dreamed of causing a breach between mother and child. He would marry the girl of his choice, if he had to wait seven years like

Jacob, because this was his right; he would tolerate the mother-in-law who had fought tooth and nail to defeat him, because that was his wife's duty. It was a harder and juster interpretation of life than later generations subscribed to.

But more to be pitied than the dogged suitor and the frightened bride was the worsted opponent, the resolute fighter five feet high, who made the best of it in the end and never owned she was wrong. Never able to retrace her steps into the realm of kindness, she seemed at last like a soul wandering in its self-made wilderness crying out for all she had lost, for all she had repulsed with fury — and going out into the dark, still embattled, still refusing and longing for love.

At this time life held compensations for her. The small fishing port she had first known became a large holiday resort, and in that year, 1924, the town decreed a festival to lengthen its season. This was a source of pride to Grandma, who was a councillor. She took me to see the great chain of lights making a necklace of golden beads for miles along the bay. That was a thing of beauty, but all the rest seemed very vulgar to me. Intolerant of public amusements I managed to endure the pushing crowds from the Lancashire towns and all the seaside racket only by keeping my mind on secret enjoyments of my own. The hand that stole into my blazer pocket was caressing a book — Daudet's oddly-named account of his schooldays, *Le Petit Chose* — and he went with me as a chosen companion, nearer to my mind than the cheerful crowds sucking humbugs or shouting to each other as they trailed back to the railway station. I really did not know I was being smug.

Home again in York, I listened to descriptions of Switzerland and accepted a beautiful red purse from Paris. It was September now, and I collected clothes for Oxford. The staple outfit I chose was a coat and skirt in navy blue, with braid trimming. It was rather middle-aged, but it had been bought at a shop instead of being made at home, so it had prestige in my eyes. I asked my father to paint a *Theta* on my trunk, as a means for easy recognition; no one knew that my secret pen-name began with that letter, as it was a Greek word meaning the thrumming of a lute. I married it with a French one. Why on earth did I choose that name, *Maturin Threttanelo?* I wrote the luggage labels myself, and the O of Oxford turned out so big that it made my mother catch my eye and smile.

The last Sunday came. As usual we went to church, walking up the flagged path under the lime-trees, pausing outside the wonderful porch that I had seen every week for 15 years. The signs of the Zodiac on the outside circle of the six Orders were fast decaying; one could distinguish some of them, Gemini and Pisces and Virgo, but whether the four-legged beasts were Leo or Taurus would be hard to decide. The inner orders were clearer: continuous lines of ornament and grotesque headed warriors and horned monsters of the Norman imagination. The little columns supporting them were topped by capitals telling stories, the fox and the stork for instance. I was only one of the people who had enjoyed these tales in stone during their life of 800 years.

I used to sit in the side aisle with the children to help to look after them; when they had filed out those pews were empty but for the teachers and there were no distractions to prevent me from listening to my father's sermon. He had always been worth listening to, all my life. He prepared his sermons carefully but used only skeleton notes. They were full of Biblical explanations and parallels and also full of his own spiritual experience and references to the burning questions of the day, never irrelevant and never dull. One such sermon moved me to write in my diary, *I think he is a truly great man*. It was his personal certainty which gave his words such force and penetration. He spoke simply: 'our Jesus' he said, as of somebody he knew well, and the story he had so often told became on this occasion a new event, as he found words to describe the cosmic process enacted in one short life. He told us how Jesus had emptied himself to become entire man, only to advance, to pioneer, opening up during his thirty years a new road from manhood to Godhead, 'growing,' said my father, 'as it has become possible for us to grow,' and from the beginning of his ministry reaching out more and more to the things he had left behind him. The life of Christ seen in this way became a microcosm of perfect growth, culminating in the Ascension and union with God. It was the prototype of the onward movement of the human world.

My father had never heard of Teilhard de Chardin, nor indeed had many other people at that time. His theology was no doubt largely his own, arrived at by long meditation on the Scriptures. This breadth of vision existed solely for the enlightenment Sunday by Sunday of a small group of worshippers in a humble city church. Of such unselfseeking voices is the universal Church composed, and no doubt the Kingdom of Heaven.

My own comment at the time, enthusiastic though it was, showed how far I was from that kingdom. I certainly wrote in my diary, *Heaven be praised for my grand father*, but when I went to tell him what I thought about it (an unusual step on my part) what I said was, 'If ever I do anything, I'll tell them where I get it from!' He looked at my infantile arrogance and smiled his warm smile. 'Well, we all get it together, don't we?' he said.

The day came when I sat in the train and said goodbye to my parents. The curve of the line soon wiped away my mother's look of anxious love and my father's buoyant wave of his clerical hat. Goodbye, goodbye... And also to all the other supports of youth — the comfort of friendship and the spur of admiration, the firm tramlines of discipline, and the delicate Gothic tracery which was a continual reminder of the life of the soul.

It was 1st October, and as I watched the landscape skim by, warm and mellow, the honey-coloured stubble fields and the rich gamut of golds and yellows in the woods, verses began to shape themselves in concert with the rhythmic rattle of the train.

> *Now blessings on thee, Sycamore!*
> *And all ye trees of wood and wold,*
> *Which feel the touch of Autumn sore*
> *And blush and redden into gold;*
> *And blessings be on all who take*
> *The frost of life, the rime of pain,*
> *And bid it yield, for all men's sake,*
> *Beauty that erst had latent lain...*

Was it Marchy who was in my mind? But then the lines reverted to myself, to the landscape that was coming, the country of the Scholar Gipsy, 'faint woods with distant sunlight blue', and they clamoured in excitement,

> *The golden landscape glows and spreads,*
> *The willows wind along the streams...*

It was not hard to find a rhyme for that, for at the end of the line was my dream city, waiting for the singer of this paean, who was approaching with every revolution of the well-oiled wheels.

II

In a week I was singing a very different tune.

The problem was that I had no clear ideas about Oxford. Certainly, it symbolised the importance of learning, the riches of the past, the promise of the future; I knew it housed the Shelley relics and the volumes in the Bodleian; in a word, it woke the nostalgia of the Scholar Gipsy for

> *The festal line of light in Christchurch hall...*

and latterly it had proved to contain people like the Tutor.

However, college life, for me, was something quite new. I was in fact both socially and intellectually unprepared. The discrepancies in social background took me by surprise, though I did not at first recognise them for what they were. I felt only the other girls were, in manifold mysterious ways, different from myself. Some of them, very little older, seemed to have lived for centuries in this puzzling world. Their fathers were politicians, writers, people whose names were known; one was the daughter of the Speaker of the House, another of a world-famous pianist, another had a title. Their clothes were different, the way they composed their faces or styled their hair was different. They talked among themselves about things and people of which I was totally ignorant. Most significantly of all, these young women had been to boarding-school. I did not realise at the time why the freshman year divided itself up in so definite a way — but it became apparent that it grouped according to the types of school represented. Eventually, I was duly to fit into a small group of girls from independent schools, that is, between the group from the great boarding-schools and those who had come along the State route.. But this segregation was quite veiled to me on first arrival. In dire perplexity I weltered in the crowd, blessing the little Latin mistress who had sent me a postcard on the first day, saying: 'I know how nice it is to find someone using your Christian name!' True, in those days we used surnames for a surprisingly long time.

There were other unexpected conventions, smaller but hazardous just the same. For example, on one of the first days, I appeared in my new navy costume, to be greeted with cries of commiseration: 'You poor thing! Have you got an exam already?'

A dark suit, it became clear, was examination uniform, so it was impossible to wear it on any other occasion; the new costume languished in the wardrobe for nearly all the rest of its life.

Almost at once I found out something which unnerved me — that I had no idea how to spend money. It was necessary to buy some crockery and a bed-cover. I bought the cheapest possible, trembling at the expense. For four shillings I bought a small manicure set and felt consumed with guilt. Then — I lost my head and bought a large luxurious pair of bellows to blow up the coal fire in my room; quite unnecessary — most people used their academic gowns and proudly exhibited the holes burnt in the back. I had in fact no definite allowance and was not sure how far money would go; it was spending in the dark.

More profound and less ephemeral was my unexpected reaction against the prevailing critical spirit. This iconoclastic attitude is a feature of Oxford at any time and in the early twenties it was exaggerated. The Great Divide had happened, perhaps the Great War acting as a catalyst, and the consequences were becoming clearly noticeable. Everything met with sharp criticism: 'old-fashioned' virtues, especially patriotism, were the targets. I was going through a period of wanting to see the 'good' in everything, an attitude which provoked scorn in certain quarters; it was intensely unfashionable.

Thus, for me there was a curious emptiness about life. The goal had been reached, the tension in consequence now relaxed — and what did one find? All this coming and going, what was it all about? All these lectures and classes, societies, coffee-parties and boating trips, what did they all add up to? There must be some central spring to the mechanism but it was difficult to detect. Probably there was also some weariness in me, after all those years of striving.

Work alarmed me. It was one thing to be good at school, far away in the North; here they were all picked people and it stood to reason that things would be different. Even an encouraging comment on a paper failed to convince me. My tutor, of course, always made life simple again, by transferring confidence, but for two terms it was to be work for Pass Moderations, and this involved other teachers. The worst thing was that this disorientation threatened to drive out poetry. The fear of 'drying up' was always at the back of my mind and the conflict with which I had for so long been preoccupied — that between the creative and intellectual sides of the mind was in fact intensified by the critical atmosphere. Maybe it was to be expected that one would have no friends. But what if one were never to hear again that familiar voice, life's companion so far?

When I went to lectures on Logic, held for the girls in a room at the top of the Clarendon Building, my eye was caught by a little thorn-tree growing beside the stone steps in front of the massive portico. It still had a few bright leaves, and it seemed to be a friend. It was the only living thing against the austere background of grey stone and it looked like a fountain of refreshment.

The fact that this course was for women only underlines the segregation which, though just coming to an end, was still prevalent. Chaperone rules existed, and I was disapproved of by more advanced spirits for naïvely expecting to keep them. Chaperones in the flesh were a mythical race and I never saw one, but it was laid down to the girls (not to the men) that tête-à-tête parties in men's rooms were not allowed, that there must be two girls in any mixed party and so on and so on. It was in my third term that things were improved by the production of a 'little grey book' which was handed out to men and women alike on matriculation. The rules in that, though unbelievably stiff as seen from a later day, were a little better. The Principal gathered us all together to explain them, and when she had painstakingly gone over all the occasions when it was a misdemeanour to be alone with the opposite sex, she paused, looked at us over the top of her spectacles — she, the lofty, distant and impressive — and remarked, 'It says *nothing* about country walks!'

Rules did not worry me, nor the absence of the male element, which had anyway always been absent, nor the necessity of asking for late leave and being in by eleven o'clock. All that was simple. But I had one definite and real trouble. My weakness in not making an initial decision about the Training Grant was now coming home to roost. The Director of the Training Department for Teachers notified me that I had qualified for the grant, and was invited to present myself at the office in North Oxford on the second Saturday of Full Term and there sign the undertaking that I intended to teach after taking my degree.

Here was the approach of Nemesis. I was still undecided. Teaching as a career, teaching in the abstract, filled my soul with boredom and alarm. Why, since my experience of teachers had been so favourable? Was it, as I thought, because teaching required one to attend more to method than to matter, to scholars than scholarship? Or because I felt my inadequacy and limited field of vision, and dare not think of staying within the restricted walls of a school? Would it not be stronger, more honest, to stick to my guns and refuse the grant?

I talked about it to no one, sought no advice, least of all from the people at home. The tutor, consulted later on, did suggest a loan from the College, but the idea of a burden of debt was just as bad; it seemed so unlikely that I would ever earn any money, that commodity I had observed as being so hard to come by in the world. Struggling on with the dilemma I kept a non-committal face turned to the invading world. Feeling, not thought, swung me hither and thither like something on the tide, and the resulting paralysis was agony.

At last it was the very day of the meeting, and on the crest of the latest wave I decided to refuse the grant and stay away. I wrote a letter and gave it to one of the girls who was to attend the meeting. Somewhat surprised, she accepted the commission, and I stayed behind.

That should have given me peace, but it was the prelude to the stormiest weekend I had ever known. The others came back, comfortable and contented; the Director had given them a friendly little sermon and they settled down to work with their vocation as a perspective. But my brave front began to crack; my independence gave way to misery and terror. Had I done right? How could I know? The next verses after the burst of optimism in the train were very different.

> *Speak, for Thy servant heareth, day by day*
> *Stretching forth arms that yearn, and hands that pray,*
> *For stars are dim, and night surrounds my way.*
>
> *Speak, for Thy servant heareth, hour by hour*
> *Beholding fading leaf and falling flower,*
> *For all must change, save Thine immortal power.*
>
> *Speak, for Thy servant heareth; now at last*
> *Ripen the fruit that blossomed in the past,*
> *Though petals needs must fall, and wither fast.*

Speak, yes, but how to detect the true voice?

Sunday was a nightmare. I cannot recollect what happened in the morning; probably I went to the Cathedral, uncomforted for once by its creamy luminousness, the marriage of fan-vaulting and interlaced arcades, the shaft of light across the clerestory. Perhaps I picked up the anthem-book and read for the first time the little poem which was to haunt me for so long as an apt description of my inner life:

Insanae et vanae curae
Invadunt mentes nostras,
Saepe furore replent
Corda privata spe.
Quid prodest, O mortalis,
Conari pro mundanis,
Si coelos negligis?
Sunt fausta tibi cuncta
Si Deus est pro te.

That afternoon I had been invited to a freshers' tea, but was too dispirited to go. So it was a lonely Sunday. In the evening there was no dinner in College, only a cold supper called 'Nondies'. So it was possible to go to Evensong. I went to the nearest church; Sunday had always been a day of churchgoing. At home it would be Harvest Festival, but here in the South it was over. I sat at the back, in a corner behind a pillar, which turned out to be a good thing, for the effect of the familiar chants on my overwrought mind was devastating, and I began to cry. I sat there with the tears running down my face; fortunately no one noticed.

It had never occurred to me that I would be homesick, and the nature of that dreadful sickness, that spiritual measles, was unknown and unguessed to me. It has a violent effect of constriction in the breast, quite physical. It is impossible to believe that in a week or two one will be the normal self again. And I had an additional burden to bear, the revelation of what home meant in more general ways. If life in College seemed trivial and meaningless, because it was being lived by a crowd of young people all bent on their own concerns, it was largely because I was missing not only my home, but the parish. I, indeed, I who had been let off everything, who had done so little for others, content to live with my books and my dreams among the poplars, roses and syringa of the Rectory garden, while the tide of suffering washed up to the door! Compared to the gaiety of the girls in the College, privileged beings after all, the people in the parish seemed unfinished, helpless before their fate, such as the pale children, or the organist whose shambling legs ruined by polio still managed to find the pedals and make music. They were real people and that life was real — extraordinarily balanced between rare beauty in the old city and in books, and the strong realities of need and sacrifice and service. I had been living by proxy, but I now dimly understood how rich a life it had been.

I went back to Nondies and my quiet room with a mind illuminated and cleansed by tears. Things looked different now. I knew it was not possible to take money from my father, to make him pay because I would not be bound. It was just not possible.

Next day I wrote another letter to the Director to tell him I had changed my mind. A laconic reply fixed an appointment for the following

Wednesday. I presented myself at the tall red-brick house, and the declaration was put before me. I signed it.

'It says you agree to teach — but, you see, it doesn't say for how long,' pointed out the quiet kind man who had spread out the document in front of me.

Another man was present, a younger one, who looked at me with friendly eyes. Neither of them suggested by word or manner that there had been anything odd in my conduct. Only the young man said to the other, 'Miss Mann is something of a poet, I believe.' And his manner was perfectly serious.

Locked in my private world, I said nothing and hurried away, but with the feeling that I had been well treated. There was nothing embarrassing in the way they had accepted my return. But how did they know about the poetry? It was all perplexing and mysterious. It did not occur to me that they might have contacted the tutor, and heard her understanding diagnosis of the odd little case.

Anyway, that was done: the first concession to the necessities of life. I walked back to the College, kicking my feet through the heaps of autumn leaves. At the gate I paused and looked in. It was tea-time, and nobody was about but the porter's little white dog basking in the autumn sunshine. There it was, the College where at present I had not a single friend. But friends *were* there, hidden in the future. All sorts of experiences lay within those walls and beyond them, even the friendship of Erasmus.

It must not be supposed that I saw this day's work as a victory or a noble sacrifice. It was a relief, but it was also a defeat. I had failed to stand by my convictions, to 'burn my boats'. I had chosen the safe way instead of committing myself to Providence as the swimmer throws himself into the sea. In a sense I had perjured my soul, promising for the sake of money to enter on a profession which should only be taken up with a sense of vocation. I had bowed to the world.

He ne'er is crowned
With immortality, who fears to follow
Where airy voices lead!

Jolted to the bottom of my soul I stood looking at the College gate. It *was* a new life which was opening, but it did not seem to be the glorious imaginary one I had sketched for myself with every thought of Oxford. Although I had known it would mean relinquishing the leading-strings, standing on one's own feet, I had not at all understood how weak those feet were. Here I was, tottering towards a future, which now looked bleak and schoolmistressy, while the airy spirit of Poetry clapped its wings in derision and flew away, leaving its unworthy votary standing in the Woodstock Road.

It was not so bad as that, of course. There would still be verse. And Oxford would come up to scratch, opening its treasury of books and talk and friendship. The illumination was to be felt in rapturous snatches; the dream was to be fulfilled — in the late night talks by the fireside, or in the slow punt drifting between banks of moon-daisies under the dipping willows; or in the map of the human spirit which pieced itself together out of the pages of books. Always, too, there would be misgivings, a cyclic return of self-mistrust. Then the beckoning mirage would reappear:

Pass the gates of Luthany, tread the region Elenore.

I belonged to a generation which saw a division in the mind, putting a fence between the work of the intellect and the creative life. To make it whole again was a task beyond my small powers, or even to join in the rehabilitation of English that was the work of the poets of my time. But my limited life held a pale reflection of these universal problems, and my load of guilt was a sharing with the whole world. I had no idea of this in those early days, but I did strive to bear what imagination and sensibility inflicted on me. I knew that 'unreality' must now be banished, as with proxy loves, but the poetic voice was still there. And from time to time, in an agony of lucidity, I would be granted a sight of all that was wrong, selfish, false or shoddy in the way I had lived: a shaft of light, destructive yet vivifying. *Dominus illuminatio mea.*

> *We haste away, we haste away from thee,*
> *Great shadow of the Once-dreamed, still undone,*
> *Our life's sweet terror, and all-searching sun.*
>
> *How small beside thee seem our petty joys!*
> *Our griefs are but thy shadow, thrown along*
> *The pathway where thy step resounds like song.*
>
> *Noise of the world is fainter in our ears*
> *Than thy strange whisper, oft importunate,*
> *That truer self must turn to, soon or late.*
>
> *Beloved pursuer, fine unresting foe,*
> *If but the strongest hearts thou vanquishest,*
> *The weaker also cry,* Give us no rest.

York College Chapel, dedicated 1960.